Barefoot in November

Parenting the Summerhill way

Zoë Neill Readhead

PRINCIPAL OF SUMMERHILL SCHOOL

Title: *Barefoot in November. Parenting the Summerhill way*
ISBN: 978-1-5272-9695-4
All text: © Worldwide Copyright Zoë Neill Readhead 2021
Published by: the A. S. Neill Summerhill Trust
(Registered Charity No. 1089804)

Edited by: Mark Vaughan
Designed by: Cathy McKinnon www.cathymckinnondesign.co.uk
Cover and illustrations by: © Katy Streeter www.katyillustreeter.com
Index by: Fiona Firth
Printed by: Pure Print

£10.00
Proceeds from the sale of this book go to the A. S. Neill Summerhill Trust,
Summerhill School, Westward Ho, Leiston, Suffolk, IP16 4HY, UK.
www.summerhillschool.co.uk

Dedication

This book is for Tony, my husband, without whom there would certainly no longer be a Summerhill today.

Dear Neill,

You were the first man in my life. You taught me how to love and what to look for in all people – humour, warmth, strength and humanity.

You gave me Summerhill and everything it stands for – it set the standard by which I would live my life and rear my children. Through many trials and tribulations, I have remained optimistic and loved the world and the people in it. I hope that I have been able to pass on what you taught me to some people ...

Remembering Rosie, Posie, John and Lon who eventually went down the plughole in our bath, Mr Wise Owl and Mr Silly Owl and how every book you read to me had to begin with: 'Once upon a time there were four little rabbits, and their names were Flopsy, Mopsy, Cottontail and Peter ...'

Although you would find today's world a mystery, I wish you could be here. I miss you so very much.

Summerhill School
founded by A. S. Neill in 1921

Contents

Introduction

I think that my circumstances and thus my experience of child-rearing may well be unique. I was born and raised at Summerhill and have stayed closely involved with it all of my life. After raising four children in the fashion that I absorbed from my father's methods and as a former Summerhill pupil myself, I have continued working, living and learning about the school and the people in it throughout my adult life. This has given me a unique opportunity to watch the way children in this rare environment grow and develop unfettered by adult expectations and surrounded by the freedom that Summerhill offers.

The thoughts that I put down here are purely my own observations and beliefs but I feel confident that what I have seen is a broad spectrum of childhood that probably nobody else living has had the privilege to see. I have been a pupil, a parent, a grandparent and for the past 36 years, the Principal of Summerhill School. I have watched children living free-range in a self-governing, self-regulating environment for most of my life. This has been an amazing joy and I feel honour bound to share some small part of what I have learned from it.

Summerhill might be a kind of blueprint for family life. This book attempts to draw on my Summerhill experience, extract some stories and conclusions, and pass them on to the wider world in the sincere belief that this is an excellent and life-supporting gesture towards the complex and rewarding role of parenting.

Summerhill is a happy place to live, it gives adults and children a special relationship and it finishes off by sending the most amazing young people out into the world with a deep experience of democratic education, a richer emotional intelligence than they might have got elsewhere, and full of confidence and self-awareness. If we can look closely at what Summerhill does and how it does it, then perhaps we can transfer some of what it offers into our homes, into our parenting. I believe it can help many families find a more peaceful and harmonious life together and take some of the strain out of the everyday stresses of school life for the children.

Throughout this book, you will find that I may repeat myself — my apologies — but if I say it more than once, it is important and you absolutely cannot say important things too often!

One last point for this introduction is that I fully recognise that many children and young people are raised by carers, not their biological parents. In this book, my use of the word parents covers both parents and carers.

Parents

I love parents. I love seeing them out with their children at supermarkets, in the park, at the zoo. I have such respect for the fact that people are ready to change their whole lives for that little scrap of a person who arrives with such a flourish of trumpets and proceeds to take over everything! People that you may always have thought of as self-indulgent, or self-centred or a bit on the lazy side — they will slip into night feeds, colicky crying and all the long, drawn-out daily practices such as wrapping up little children to go out, packing up the car for ages to make a simple shopping trip and being totally unable to have a personal life as it was before. Nothing short of heroic, really!

I heard a great quote about small children the other day — *'like short, violent storms in a clear blue sky'* — the way they go from oh-so-happy to absolutely enraged or sad within a few minutes.

Small children are like short, violent storms in a clear blue sky.

I thought it was a wonderful description and expresses an awful lot about life with a toddler.

Unfortunately, the passion that drives parents to love and care for their children can mean that they over-think the process of parenting. Their deep emotional attachment often blurs many of the more sensible and fundamental realities of living together as a family. Parents can often allow their own fears and worries to cloud their children's lives or their own aspirations to cast unfair demands upon them.

I well remember the unexpected and overpowering passion that gripped me as I looked upon my newborn first child, a daughter, Amy. It frightened me a little. I would find myself thinking about awful scenarios where somebody came to harm her. I had to work hard to move away from such thoughts. They were unproductive and only

I have such respect for people ready to change their whole lives for that little scrap of a person.

tortured me. But I knew that if anybody had come to my house and in any way threatened my child, I would have mercilessly pulled them limb from limb.

This passion can be very harmful in our relationship with our children. We must recognise it, accept it and then tuck it away as firmly as we can. We must try to come to our parenting with a clean canvas — to start again without our worries or the shadows of our past lives. We must try to move away from our relationships with our own parents and teachers and our own fears and rages about life. Children need to create their own lives and personalities without us starting the painting on the canvas with our picture of the world.

At Summerhill, we often see the side of parenting that has gone awry. This can happen very quickly and causes much stress and unhappiness to everybody involved. So many doubts and questions arise that it can make a difficult job even harder than it needs to be. It can also lead to some very dark and challenging places.

It strikes me that we are usually looking at the wrong things in our preparations for becoming parents. We tend to worry about how having a baby will affect us, take responsibility, deal with the daily life of having a child and the sleepless nights; what will we do when the baby cries? How will we react if our child misbehaves in public? What about when they go to school, will they be clever or find learning difficult?

We tend not to think about the most important thing, which is what we, as individual people, will bring to the table and how we will adapt ourselves to being parents. We ought to be thinking about things like — Am I an anxious person, and if I am, will I find it difficult not to project this upon my child?

How will this anxiety affect my ability to be a 'good' parent, an effective parent?

Am I naturally a very tense person? Will this have a negative effect on family life? Will I create a tension in the air by this very tension in myself?

Am I passive or strong? If I am passive then I will need to gain some more assertive skills in order to 'manage' a family (and believe me, a family certainly needs to be managed, though not in the conventional way that most people would imagine). If I am a strong-willed person who likes to have my own way, then I might need to think about how I will react to the compromises that I will have to make as a parent. How will my own characteristics affect the children, and how can I minimise this?

What impact can these things — our personality traits and life history — have upon our children as they grow up?

Once we have recognised any problems that we have, then it is much easier to see how they might affect the process of rearing our children. There will be many things that we should be considering so that we can try to put things in place to assist us rather than to let our emotional difficulties take over and cause their own problems.

We need to think about ourselves as people and find ways to be less tense, less anxious, less demanding, less full of expectations of family life and our new child. This will take a lot of thought, self-discovery and some self-discipline, so the earlier we begin, the better.

All of us need to prepare to be parents; by that, I do not mean buying baby clothes or getting ready for the sleepless nights or worrying about whether our child says 'please' or 'thank you'. We need to go much deeper and begin looking at the critical things that can help to make us better parents.

We need to work on how to control our own anxieties, how to remain calm. Perhaps we will need to work on being more assertive and how best we will show strong but entirely fair direction to our child. We need to face and recognise our own fears and prejudices to minimise what we off-load onto our child and try to ensure that we never think of our own past family emotions in our requirements. Far too many parents try to compensate for their own upbringing, which they felt was too dominating, by giving their children free rein to do whatever they want to do. It is so important to remember that being assertive and in control of family life is not being bossy or authoritarian; it is just good management — that's all.

We need to get our priorities right and think about the big picture in an unsentimental way, not about whether they are eating their greens, whether they have had a routine bath today or if they said a 'bad' word while playing cards with their grandad. Trying to impose rules about all those things only creates an environment of bickering and lack of trust. What is important is that your child is a reasonable person, that they can take responsibility for things that they do and say, that they care about the world and the people in it, that they know things are sometimes not perfect. Also, that they can deal with that without grumbling or having a hissy fit.

These things they will learn from you. Not because you have taught them but because this is who you are, and they can see it every day in you and your family environment.

This is also why it is essential to have a wider group of family and friends and for you and them to know it is okay to share a bit of your parenting too. So often, people close to us are too polite or afraid to put their point of view forward or get involved with our children in anything other than chit-chat. Children need a lot of input from many people who are not their parents, on all sorts of subjects. If they don't, then they are only getting a one-sided view of life. Remember that older children outside the family can be full of wisdom and common sense, and they still remember what being a small child was like.

We need to give a lot of thought to how we can be equal partners in our family relationships, treat each child with love and approval without sentimentality, and talk to them with respect and kindness, just as we would with our best friend. Finally, but significantly, we need to ensure that we retain a great sense of humour and more than a bit of silliness.

I have been parent watching for over forty years, interacting in different ways with hundreds of families. I have seen them all, those who love their children too much, those who love them too little, those who think they know best and those who are in despair because through all their love and endeavour, things are going terribly, terribly wrong, and they just do not know how to put them right.

A child will come to Summerhill at any age from five years but probably no later than 12. After a time, what makes changes in these families is not because the child is going to Summerhill, but because in doing so, they are absorbing and building for themselves many of the fair, common-sense communication, negotiation and compromise skills that they learn naturally through living in this well-balanced community of children and adults from many different countries and backgrounds. These skills then become part of the child's own family, and very often parents report that their children are teaching them, which is an enlightening learning experience as well as bringing a new balance into the household.

So, let us get back to looking at what it is that Summerhill does for a child and just how you might use it in a family's daily life.

I think we need to establish, after looking at Summerhill, that the most vital part of being a good parent must be the ability to let your children be without you. We have to repeat it often — daily would be best — that our children do not belong to us and, more importantly, they owe us nothing. I may say this quite a lot in these following pages, but please bear with me. It is just such a powerful and important thing to know about our relationship with our children that we cannot say it too often!

We must be able to step back, let them get on with their lives and try to be a shepherd rather than a trainer. It is difficult to do this in a home environment because we are on top of one another all the time. But with a lot of thought, planning, and certainly a lot of self-evaluation and self-discipline, it is possible to give children this kind of freedom and lack of expectation. By analysing the strengths of what Summerhill is giving the children, we can find ways of emulating it in our homes.

I have to emphasise once again that we must not allow our own weaknesses, anxieties, prejudices or aspirations to step into our family life and take control of our child-rearing. We need to keep a cool head, think about what we want to do and let our fears remain our fears and not become family fears.

Raising a family

Bringing up children is not a task; it is an adventure — a learning experience for both parties. Children need to learn about the world and the people in it, and parents need to know how best to help them negotiate these sometimes stormy seas. Our role is to be loving and supportive and to shepherd children through the learning process as best we can, whilst keeping a low profile and allowing them to be themselves. A shepherd does not try to control or change the way her sheep behave, she allows them to be sheep, but she has to keep them safe and to look after their welfare whilst they are under her care, which means that she will have to move them from field to field to protect them from predators or bring them in for dipping or lambing. This is not curtailing their freedom but is keeping them safe and well.

Of course, in our child-rearing we will all make some mistakes along the way — but imagine if you were teaching somebody to dance. What you would do is to show them the steps, take them in your arms — and start dancing. What you would not do is dominate them, humiliate them or shout at them whenever they took a step wrong, nor, very importantly, would you let them stamp upon your feet and demand that you go faster, slower or do it the way they want you to do it.

In a well-balanced family, the adults and children have equal respect whilst having very different roles. It is sometimes difficult for parents to understand just how many rights they, themselves also need. Life can be so geared up to the children that it is easy to forget to take time out for yourselves. Children need to learn about respecting other people's quiet time and knowing when they have to step away, and give adults a bit of space.

I have seen many situations where the children were, frankly, behaving like spoiled brats, but their parents fail to see this. They will proudly think that the child is emotionally free and creative, wherein my eyes, they are just impolite and interrupting our adult conversation. Even free-range children have to learn the basics, just as we adults need to know them. I will not interrupt your game or try to control it, but then neither can you interrupt my conversation and try to dominate it. By all means, feel free to ask a question or make a short comment, but then you must get on with what you are doing and leave this conversation to us. I cannot tell you how many times I have watched children totally dominate their parents. Sadly I do not think that the parents even noticed it.

Growing up takes a long time — there are no 'quick fixes.' There will be times when you despair of your children ever getting up in the morning or taking out the rubbish. But it will happen. One day they will be 25, and you will just swell with pride at the wonderful young people they have become.

The most crucial ingredient of all on this journey is to remain calm and respectful, keep a good (and probably quite bizarre) sense of humour and have fantastic fun. There is nothing more satisfying and delightful than to be part of a growing family, no matter how exhausting it is!

Living in Summerhill as Principal for over thirty-five years has enabled me to watch many children arrive young and small and grow up into young adults. They have all come from different countries, different families and different child-rearing practices. I have seen many things that work well and many that are really not successful at all. This will always show itself in the way the child is, how they behave and how they approach life in general. It is not irreversible but sometimes needs some hard work and big changes in approach and action by their parents at home as well as for the community at school.

A particular yardstick for each of us at Summerhill is to take responsibility for our own actions. It is one of the school's founding principles. Freedom not Licence — or freedom with responsibility. In this modern age where both individuals and society as a whole seem quite unable to do this simple thing without constantly expecting it to be somebody else's fault, this is of the utmost importance.

Freedom means personal freedom, the ability to choose for ourselves the things that are our own business and not for anybody else to decide, such as whether we might want tea or coffee for breakfast, which passions we shall pursue and whether we would like the wardrobe or the desk under the window in our bedroom. On the other hand, licence would be the things that affect other people, such as playing drums at three in the morning, pulling the cat's tail, or using somebody's computer or bike without their permission.

Another issue that often raises its head is this: Most parents think they need to give their children lots of attention all of the time. But do you know — one of the main things that kids love about Summerhill is that they do not get grown-ups around them all the time? We can always tell the new children because they are the ones that hover around us, hoping to be amused or played with. When they have been here for a while, they just cycle past and carry on going with a casual 'Hi'!

Summerhill freedom means being able to play on your own with your friends and siblings, sorting out your differences by yourselves (within reason, of course), discovering the world and the delights that are in it, being creative in as off-beat or bizarre a manner as you can contrive, not being judged, or people having expectations of you, and, if you want, going barefoot in November …

It is very easy to shower one's children with affection and stimulus. It is such fun and gives us a lot of pleasure too, watching them learning, engaging with them. But therein a danger lurks, that of giving the children too much attention.

A fun engagement can quickly turn into a situation where children begin to live in an adult world. They will find it harder to amuse themselves and to enjoy their own pleasure in what they do because they are so accustomed to getting feedback, mostly very positive, from the adults around them. We see this sometimes at Summerhill, where children can find living their own lives a bit boring or even frightening as they have been so used to adults interacting with them. It can take a while for them to find their way and learn to stand on their own feet.

Let the kittens play, enjoy and learn about life. Let them tumble out of the box to be silly, cry, laugh, and enjoy each other's company, but mostly just let them be. Children reared this way do not have 'Toddler Tantrums', 'Terrible Twos' or 'Teenage Rebellion'. At the end of it all, you will have the very best friends that you can have. People whom you know most intimately and who know you intimately as well, having all shared a childhood of love, honesty, some tears and plenty of laughter. Never, never forget the laughter!

Summerhill School

A. S. Neill wrote:
'The future of Summerhill itself may be of little import. But the future of the Summerhill idea is of the greatest importance to humanity. New generations must be given the chance to grow in freedom. The bestowal of freedom is the bestowal of love. And only love can save the world.'

A proven schooling philosophy and system

After 36 years of being at the helm of Summerhill School, I am amazed that the general world of education does not appear to have made a connection between the kind of academic pressures that most children have to endure in their schools and often in their homes, and the large number of young people diagnosed with severe anxiety or depression. In my view, this amounts to a form of maltreatment that in any other group of people would be considered both discriminatory and unacceptable.

Summerhill School was founded in 1921 by Neill, a Scotsman from Forfar. It has been a controversial idea from the very start, and many people would disagree with the educational philosophy behind it. The reason that I am referring to this philosophy here is that the very nature of the place with its freedom and self-regulation and its strong community spirit has enabled us to learn a lot about raising children. We have discovered how children thrive when they can have real control in their lives and that many of the problems which create unhappy youngsters or rebellious teenagers need not occur if things are managed differently.

Summerhill is a school where the pupils and adults live together as equals. There is a clear understanding among us all that we will have different roles and different needs as each child grows and matures but that the adults are in a position of responsibility and care.

Self-government and Meetings

The daily life of the school is run through democracy, using school gatherings or Meetings where the community decides upon the day-to-day life and rules by which we all live. This democracy in education is straightforward. I liken it to a group of friends who have a football to play with, and the most simple and obvious way to decide which game to play, either football or volleyball, would be to have a show of hands. This is all that our democracy is. It has no special significance and does not follow a particular model of democracy — it is simply a group of people voting on the best way to deal with this specific problem at this particular time, which works wonderfully for all of us. Regularly, the quality of discussion in the whole group and the subsequent decision-making by the Meeting reveals an astounding level of insight, which produces solutions to the community's current issues being dealt with at that time.

It is also the medium by which we learn how to live in harmony with other people. Obviously, there will be misdemeanours in a school, differences of opinion, cases of minor bullying, and sometimes something more serious that needs to be addressed, such as people being woken and kept awake at night.

At Summerhill, adults may well wade in to try and resolve a dispute or tell children they are doing something out of line, but this also applies to all members of the community. So, an older child or one of your own group might call an adult to task for misbehaving, breaking a school rule or upsetting somebody. We have Ombudsmen elected by ballot, who are available to help mediate if there are problems. They have to have been in the school for two years to qualify, both adults and children. An Ombudsman can confiscate something or ban you temporarily from a certain area until the next school Meeting, but mostly they are just the voice of common sense to calm things and find out what really happened. They can also help younger or more shy pupils bring a case to the school Meeting and act as witnesses.

The community works as a unit of many ages and experiences, and because of the lack of enforced discipline, conflict between adults and children is rare. Differences will be most noticeable in a school Meeting when everybody is voting for a late bedtime on a party night. The youngsters will almost always all vote for the 4 am slot, while we oldies tend to go for a nice early one — and generally lose the vote!

This system can, at first, sound like complete anarchy where the children rule the roost and do whatever they want, but nothing could be further from the truth; as stated earlier, we run on the solid founding principle of 'Freedom not Licence' or freedom with responsibility. This means that all of the pupils learn, through a gradual process, that one cannot do whatever one wants to do in life, that we have to respect one another and that personal freedom is that which does not affect the freedom of somebody else. Within these areas, we have seen that, despite what would generally be expected, children are capable of making decisions about things that happen in their lives with the support and guidance of the school community.

The school currently has around 400 rules in the law book. These cover many aspects of life, from what time pupils go to bed at night to how many may use the trampoline safely at the same time. Many of them are tailor-made to fit a particular situation and may be dropped at a later date when no longer needed. They are all made by community vote and can be amended by anybody bringing a case to the school Meeting. In a large group of as many mixed ages as we have at the school, it is easy to build up a lot of rules in a comparatively short time. Of course, there are many more than you would need in any family home!

A. S. Neill wrote:
'At Summerhill, the pupils would fight to the death for their right to govern themselves. In my opinion, one weekly General School Meeting is of more value than a week's curriculum of school subjects'.

This is still true today. Now held thrice weekly, they are the forum in which we discuss issues, make, drop or change laws and govern our day-to-day lives.

Living as we do, in a largely boarding community plus some day pupils, it is most important that we have safety nets and expectations regarding behaviour towards one another. Thus anybody can bring a case to the Meeting for help, to complain, or sometimes just because they are angry. Issues are discussed and resolved with great openness and honesty. The fines voted by the Meeting generally tend to fit the crime and vary from, perhaps, a twenty-four-hour screen ban, missing a swimming session, a job for the community or a small money fine.

There is an elected chair, a new one every second Meeting, and a secretary who writes the minutes and takes cases for the agenda. Chairing the Meeting is no easy task. You have to be assertive, confident, aware of the cases but still impartial, and able to control around 70 pupils and staff. Our school laws say that the chair has 'ultimate power' so they are able to move people if they are disturbing the proceedings, ask them to leave, call them to attend for a case against them or even close the Meeting if it is too long or gets a bit rowdy, which is very rare indeed. A good, experienced chair will always call a small child's hand so that they do not have to wait (they might want to wee, for instance) and allow a certain amount of leeway while being very strict with the older ones and adults, making sure they have to ask to leave and get permission before doing so!

Everybody has an equal right to be heard and to vote. New children come into our school Meeting with very little confidence in their ability in this field. They tend to sit and listen and start tentatively putting their hands up in the vote, often just going along with their friends or watching an adult. However, it does not take long before they are vigorously voting for what they want.

Sometimes, when they have been at the school for a few months, they will start voting against everything that is proposed. This can be a sort of 'rite of passage' for some children. It is a fantastic learning experience. You can often see a mischievous glint in their eye as they make use of their new power.

'I don't care what the proposal is; I am just going to vote against it — because I can!'

We sometimes have visitors to Summerhill from children's councils in other schools. They say that in their school the one thing they are not able to do is to make decisions about the little things that affect them every day. They are asked to discuss many 'adult' themes but what they actually want is to talk about what clothes they can wear, do they need a uniform and why? Can they choose the biscuits they get at tea time? These are the things that matter to them.

We had a mediator who was observing an Ofsted inspection at Summerhill. He was from the Institute of Education in London and was a long-time supporter of the school. After the General School Meeting, he was rather disappointed because the children had been discussing whether they could drink fizzy drinks in the school library or not. He felt sure that at Summerhill the children would have been talking about more fundamental issues and perhaps world affairs rather than be so trivial. But most of our school Meetings are about things that one might term as 'housekeeping'. Mundane sounding things that affect us and matter to all of us every day. Was there too much noise in the House area last night? Who has been taking the pegs off the peg-board (our school sign-out system) and scattering them around the place? Why not pick up the rubbish you leave after playing in the San area field and pick up your jumpers rather than leaving them on the grass!

Summerhill Meetings are the very heart of the school. They are practical, down-to-earth, humorous, sometimes a bit boring, but mostly absolutely wonderful to watch. After over 70 years of association with Summerhill, I try never to miss a Meeting.

Lessons

Part of the Summerhill self-regulation is the complete freedom to attend classes or not. This is very radical stuff and not for every family. But it would be a shame to cast off the whole system because one did not understand it. I hope that I can show the value of this lack of compulsion to attend lessons and the reasoning behind it; this genuine freedom to play or go to classes began with Neill in 1921, and it's been the same ever since. In Summerhill, we live in an equal community; this equality is a fundamental part of how it works, adults and children together. You cannot have a self-governing community where everybody has equal rights if you then tell the children that they have to go to certain classes or learn certain things. Technically, the school Meeting could do this, but it has never come up, though we did briefly consider it once when it looked as though the government was intending to try and close the school in 1999. But that, as they say, is another story ...

While Summerhill children have the personal freedom to follow their own needs, the professional staff of around 17 teachers and house parents provide, what is in effect, a bespoke education. The pupils have absolute freedom to attend classes or not. They can prepare for and sit the UK national examinations — GCSE — or concentrate on other passions such as art, woodwork, science, music, or just playing outside in the rain.

In most countries there is a conventional and accepted way that children are educated. We all know this process, for most of us have been in a 'normal' school. For some, it can be an enlightening process that they enjoy, but for many children, it can be a stressful and overall unhappy experience where they learn, day in and day out, that they are failures. They know they must be failures because they find the work hard and struggle with it while imagining that everybody else is probably finding it easy. Starting your young life by feeling that you are a failure is a terrible burden to carry.

What we have discovered at Summerhill over the last hundred years is that learning need not follow the often punitive pattern that society expects it to follow.

In conventional schools, children enter at around the age of five and spend every school day in class learning things until they take their first round of exams at 16 years. The assumption is that the child will not do well academically without this opportunity or go on to further and higher education. Think of the furore that has gone on when teenagers from various countries have joined marches to demonstrate against climate change. What we heard most in the media were adults stating how terrible it is that the children were missing a whole day of school and how this could have a negative effect upon their entire future!

At Summerhill, we see a different process. Although some children will follow a fairly conventional path, others do not attend classes much for a very long time so that they can reach the age of 12 or 13 with pretty minimal skills in a conventional sense. These young people will be fields ahead in social skills and emotional balance. They will be oblique thinkers with the beginnings of passion in their interests and aspirations; the all-important 'matrix' will have been laid down in these young people to bear fruition later in life. These will be trustworthy young people able to discuss and vote upon an extensive range of social subjects and able to take real responsibility for their own actions, as well as take steps to assist other people with many shared difficulties.

At this age, they will start to think about the future, about what they plan to do after Summerhill. They will stop wanting to play all day and start to get down to work.

This is what we call self-motivation. It is the moment when you realise that you have to get on and learn stuff if you want to know it. And this is the time that you figure out it is your own responsibility to learn, not just for somebody to teach you.

It can be a difficult time at the start. Of course, in the school community, you will have experienced compulsion in various ways. Things you cannot do because they are against the school laws, such as playing computer games before three in the afternoon. Things you must do like getting up in the morning by 8:30 or going to bed at bedtime. The concept of commitment is quite familiar. But having a schedule of classes takes a bit of getting used to.

The children also need to understand and accept the idea that this work will be very demanding and will need to be taken seriously. No dropping in and out of classes if they really want to pass the exams. Teachers will be very honest with them about their progress and what needs to be done in order to go further. There is also a system of adults who look after each pupil 'After Summerhill'. They will have regular discussions during these middle years to discuss what pupils might aspire to, how to attain what they want, and suggest various ideas for colleges and other training that might be required.

A general but accurate statistic about Summerhill is that the vast majority of pupils have always attended the vast majority of lessons. The main thing is that children do get used to it, they do learn, they do pass exams, and the experience is an enriching one for them as they learn about their own ability to achieve for themselves and how to overcome difficulties with hard work and dedication. All this is supported by a professional and very caring group of adults who are skilled in the Summerhill approach to learning.

Naturally, there are some pupils who prefer not to go along the academic route but decide to do something else instead. They may be interested in practical things such as woodwork or gardening, or they may be artistic. There are many qualifications that can be taken in other areas. They may choose not to take any kind of formal qualifications at all. There is no pressure or hurry for pupils to make choices about the future; it should be entirely up to them.

So, Summerhill is not just a great big playpen. It is a planned and structured system, which allows the children to behave naturally while they are young, and then to gradually take more of an active role in both their community and in their learning and preparation for life as an adult.

The philosophy that Neill founded has been such a simple truth that there has been no need for change. It is the most natural and common-sense way to live and to educate or rear our children, almost as though this is the way nature intended we humans to be.

Education means many different things to different people. Few people will disagree that, for instance, literacy and numeracy are core values in education — but are they the only core values?

What about these:
Emotional development
Effective decision making
Creativity
Self-respect
Tolerance
Integrity
Sensitivity
Individuality
Self-motivation
Compassion and
Good old common sense

You cannot easily become an effective decision maker without being given a chance to make decisions. This must involve making mistakes from time to time as well as needing the courage to take risks, both emotional and physical. Ultimately, it means taking responsibility for the results of your actions.

These essential basics can be learned with ease in a situation where children receive respect and trust for their own judgements.

Summerhill has moved away from traditional values in education. It has structured a new way to encompass an education for the whole child, including their emotional well-being. I would argue that only schools like Summerhill can actually provide the broad and balanced curriculum demanded by the Department for Education in the UK and others around the world, because they are providing for the emotional needs of the pupils and educating the whole person with essential life skills to enable them to live, not only in harmony with others but also to contribute to the society around them.

So, a key message for families from this way of adults helping children is the importance we put on the healthy development of the emotional intelligence in every child.

Learning should not just be in the head; it must be in the heart as well. Each individual's gifts and talents, whether they are the skills to sweep stables or to become a space scientist, must be allowed to emerge and grow at their own pace and in their own time. A happy, well-balanced individual who chooses to work at everyday tasks in life is as important to society as any scholar.

A. S. Neill wrote:
'It is ludicrous that a man who can do skilled handwork should feel inferior to a university professor who may not be able to mend a puncture, ludicrous that the ploughman who can make a perfect stack or a straight furrow should rank lower in culture than a teacher.'

This expectation that everybody will achieve academically is a curse to many, many young people. It has become a kind of discrimination that should be unacceptable. We think differently about people who talk in an accepted academic way, who have degrees or letters after their names. We listen more intently when people who are 'educated' put their points of view. Why should this be the standard by which we judge people? Granted, basic literacy and a broad view of the world are important factors, but these are not necessarily gained from schoolwork. Much of it comes through social interaction and self-learning.

The late Sir Ken Robinson, champion of change in education, wrote:
'Just remember, what you do now doesn't affect the whole course of your life. It's not over till it's over. You just live your life one step at a time. You can't plan the next thing ... You can't plan the next 40 years. Do the things that interest you NOW.'

If people choose to go to university and do degrees, then for them, that is admirable. If they aspire to great learning, that is admirable too and, of course, we often need special qualifications. I had major surgery on my pancreas ten years ago; it was important to us that the surgeon was well-qualified for the job, but more importantly, and this reflects what I have been saying, I wanted to know that the surgeon who was taking a scalpel to a vulnerable part of my body was passionate about his medicine, which thankfully, he was!

There is no doubt that there are many excellent schools and many, many excellent teachers who work hard to give their pupils a broad and balanced curriculum, but how can this happen within an education system based only upon 'pass' and fail', rather than based upon the uniqueness of each individual?

A. S. Neill wrote:
'Summerhill is a happy and caring environment, but it recognises the importance of expressing emotions and learning through feelings. There is a general openness and honesty among the community members.'

Social and emotional well-being was always the critical element of Neill's philosophy. His school has continued to provide opportunities for children to govern themselves and learn social responsibility, thus ensuring that their emotional life was and is the essential aspect of all learning. He firmly believed that when a child is emotionally free, their intellect will naturally look after itself; this approach has continued at Summerhill since his death in 1973.

Neill was misrepresented by the press for most of his working life. His school was ridiculed and likened to William Golding's book 'The Lord of the Flies' on many occasions. But today, interested educators from all over the world are looking at this model of education to answer some of their own questions about what changes there need to be. Universities are studying its methods and students of education are writing their thesis on it.

Some of Summerhill's methods

In order to talk about rearing children at home and in family settings using methods that have evolved from the Summerhill School system, we need to first look at Summerhill in a bit more detail. What exactly are the lessons that we can learn from this interesting and rather astonishing place for our everyday lives?

I am not trying to sell the school, to encourage people to believe in the core philosophy of Summerhill or to think of sending their children to Summerhill, but we cannot analyse some of what it does for children and how this is achieved without looking at its methods; it's my hope that readers will find inspiration from these.

If your own children are destined for a conventional route through school and beyond, there is still a lot that can be taken from Summerhill that will be helpful in your own parenting pattern. Equality in the home does not mean that the children are in control, merely that they have a say in the way their lives will go and much more control over the things that grown-ups traditionally expect and demand from their children. For example, finding the direction that teenagers feel is their destiny can often be at odds with the expectations of parents, family and society as a whole. This generally arises from a parent's fear that their children will not be able to support themselves or make a good living. It is most often brought about through love rather than a dictatorial approach, but sadly, the end result is the same for the child and the family dynamics.

This school has been running for one hundred years. It is no longer an experiment but a working model of excellence in education and child-rearing, giving children from all different backgrounds and nationalities freedom and autonomy. As well as the majority of pupils who have come from homes where their parents would not consider there were difficulties, it has, over the years, had more than its fair share of very troubled individuals who have brought their family problems into the school and in many cases been difficult for the community to deal with. Most of the people who have attended the school have found that it was truly life-changing for them, whether their stay was a long one or a short one.

Probably the most important aspect of Summerhill, for our purpose, is that this has been a completely unique environment where children have lived and worked 'free range' without the constraints of conventional education and parenting. So, for the task of learning about a natural childhood, there cannot be a better example in the world. I firmly believe that many aspects of Summerhill's approach to children and young people are 'transferable' to 'non-Summerhill' situations in homes and schools.

I hope that by looking more closely at this approach to childhood and its methods, we can transfer something to homes and families that will be of use and will enhance family relationships. Hopefully, it can help give more young people the freedom they deserve to become true individuals, wherever this takes them, with the support and love of their families.

As you read these thoughts on education and child-rearing, you will notice that I shall not be talking much about learning, academic learning in particular. This is because actually, learning for children happens automatically. I am concerned about the children's emotional welfare and development, not their learning achievements; we offer a full curriculum and Ofsted has never found Summerhill poor or wanting in the field of academic achievements.

It is interesting that during the Coronavirus pandemic in the spring of 2020, when most children were at home and all schools closed, many parents from all over the world were reporting that their children were less stressed, happier and more creative than they had been when attending school. As parents were grappling with giving lessons to the children and finding that they just could not keep up the strict discipline needed to make them sit down and learn for the whole day, they saw, first-hand, how much better children can learn at their own speed and within their own windows of interest.

Ourselves as parents

We adults in society attach a great deal too much importance to ourselves in our relationship with children. We like to think that we are the most important people in our children's lives, and we are; they love us deeply and they need us, but we have to remind ourselves often that we are not the key players here. We alone are not the ones that make the world go around — we should merely be the shadows behind the curtain, the prompters checking the scripts who stand quietly in the wings.

People outside the family — friends, relatives, teachers and other adults are all hugely important to a child. I see this at Summerhill in the way the children respond and grow to love the adults in the community and the older children too. I think families would do well to nurture and encourage more of the outer ring of adults and older children in their lives to become more involved on a personal level. It broadens all of our experiences to share with other families and relatives and removes some of the suffocation that can become part of a life lived as a small family together every day; it could help when there are difficulties to have somebody outside the immediate family to mediate and help work out differences.

Never be afraid to ask for help from those you love and who love you — just be sure that they understand and respect your child-rearing wishes. Funnily enough, even if your family are strongly opposed to your methods, they may see something that can be helpful to you and possibly bring something to the party. Be careful not to let your own family prejudices interfere with what might be good advice just because uncle Harold is a bit of an ex-army stickler to rules and regulations!

It could be helpful to involve older children — inside and outside your immediate family circle — in the same way that our Summerhill Ombudsmen are there to assist in younger children's squabbles and disagreements, somebody who is sympathetic but not emotionally involved. It could help to take that deep personal connection out of some very emotional situations, allow things to be a bit more rational and to lose some of the family histories that often get in the way — 'You NEVER listen to me' or, 'You ALWAYS say that to me.' I am sure that most older teenagers would be very honoured to be asked to come along and have a few casual chats with an angry or confused 12-year-old — it might do untold good.

Never forget that the default setting for children is to have a proper childhood. They do not need help to do this — they can do it on their own if they are given enough time and space, without adults being around them or trying to involve themselves all of the time.

Parents who have difficulties with their children often look for other reasons, such as a medical or behaviour changing condition that might explain such problems. In my own experience, over many years working with all kinds of adults and children at Summerhill, I would say this should be the final route instead of the first one. Generally speaking, if a child is unusually disruptive or very unhappy, it can be traced to problems with nurture rather than nature, or a combination of both.

I am not in any way trying to discredit many of the conditions diagnosed, attention deficit hyperactivity disorder (ADHD) and the broad range of differences within autism being the most usual ones, but we need to find ways to lessen these problems rather than dwell upon the clinical diagnosis itself.

Too often, I have seen children and, more often, their parents use a diagnosed condition as an excuse for poor behaviour instead of seeking to rectify the difficulties.

It can look like an easy option for a child if they think they cannot behave differently. It can excuse them from a lot of things that are difficult to overcome, and it can end up as a bit of a cop-out in many families. It can also lead to low self-esteem for the whole family, with the parents feeling a sense of failure and for the child a feeling of being a victim and therefore not in control of their life, particularly when they are seeing professionals regularly. It can feel disempowering for them on many levels. It can even become a bit of a status symbol for some parents and something to make much of — exactly the wrong response, which should be to normalise and keep it at a very low profile. Whatever happens, for heaven's sake, do not keep talking about it! Interestingly, many children who attend Summerhill will opt out of their diagnosis after they have been in the school for a while, just as they might see a counsellor for a short time but very quickly want to take on their issues for themselves and will put off the sessions.

Our society is not very good at taking responsibility for things when they go wrong. Suggest to somebody that they may be making a mistake in their child-rearing and they may never speak to you again. Which, if you think about it, is crazy. This is new stuff to all of us at the start — of course we are not going to get it right every time. Think how many mistakes you made while learning to drive, or to cook or to write.

We need to be a bit humbler about our parenting skills and be ready to change direction when things are not working well. Very often, this will be all that is necessary to put something on a more even path.

Interesting that in a survey on morning TV, it was shown that in society today there is a firm understanding that if a dog misbehaves or has some kind of neurotic tendency, then it is primarily due to the owner, while if a child shows difficulties, then it is usually something inherently wrong with the child which needs fixing by a professional.

If a child is unhappy or consistently misbehaves, then the very first question I would ask is this: *'What is it that we are doing in our home with our children that could be causing this problem?'*

Somehow, we have to break down the stigma about child-rearing. We need to feel that it is okay to get it wrong. Once we think that we might have identified the problem, then we just have to shrug it off, roll up our sleeves and start trying to put things right.

Message to parents and children everywhere — *'Parents have rights too!'*

Parents don't have to rush home from work or pick up the children from school and immediately engage in providing a stimulating environment for them. They don't have to ensure that they eat a healthy diet all the time or that the children don't play outside unsupervised, or, God forbid, never let them spend time doing nothing. Parents don't have to provide stimulating pastimes and activities, drive them to ballet, swimming, visit friends, or constantly praise and show interest in everything they do. Most of all, parents don't need to engage children in stimulating conversation and make sure they are always on hand to inspire and encourage them.

It is all exhausting for the children too, who, more often than not, would prefer to just get on with their own lives and be left alone! It is also way beyond the call of duty for tired parents. You will see later that I am a great advocate for calm and quiet. Children need a calm space to get on with living without all the worry and stimulation that we adults — maybe too often — provide. As parents, we can easily talk too much, keep on about things, like conversations, and discuss things. Children do not want that. They very seldom actually discuss stuff unless they have chosen the subject and feel so inclined (how do people in the Arctic go to the toilet?), and when we listen to them, we will surely know that this is not a conversation that we want to take part in! Children also need to learn how to amuse themselves and sort out life's minor problems without us.

So why not just put our feet up, have a nice cup of tea and let everybody get on with it. It would be so much more peaceful and harmonious!

Living away from home

In looking at Summerhill as a model that we can follow in our own child-rearing to give our children more freedom and autonomy while at the same time giving them a structure in their lives that frees them emotionally, I think we should dissect what it is about the Summerhill experience that is so very successful. The first and most important thing about the school is that it is primarily a live-in community. For most modern parents this is an almost unthinkable elephant in the room. The very idea of not having their children around for a lot of the time, plus the old connotations of 'boarding schools' and everything that went with them, is shocking to the extreme.

So, let us take a look at this elephant.

To begin with, we need to acknowledge that Summerhill pupils absolutely love the boarding aspect of school life. They will generally not start to live in at the school until they are around six or seven years of age and then only when they feel ready. Before that, they will be day pupils, coming in from nine in the morning until five in the evening. They will then have a period, if they wish, to stay for a few nights each week until the family and themselves feel comfortable staying all the time. There are three weekends each term to go home or stay with friends, and the school holidays are two separate months plus eight weeks in the summer; annually, that's four months and (potentially) nine weekends not at Summerhill.

Ask any Summerhill alumni from different generations and they will all say that boarding was one of the most important things for them. It gave them ownership of their community and the ability to deal with life for themselves while always having the school democratic system, experienced adults and the other pupils to give them support and help if things went wrong. Naturally, children will miss their parents sometimes, but it need not have a deep-seated effect. The fact is that these children are leading players. They have chosen to be at the school and to share the Summerhill community. It helps build strength in them as individuals because the only way a child ever gets to attend Summerhill is because they have chosen to do so. The people at school become their village, their tribe and their family with the equivalent aunts and uncles, cousins and friends that would have shared the lives of our long-lost forefathers in days gone by.

So, bearing all of this in mind, we need to look at ways to bring this independence and calm into our children's lives when they are at home. First of all, we need to ask precisely what it is about the boarding at Summerhill that is so very special?

Our society mostly thinks of children being away from their parents as a negative thing, and in many, many cases, this is absolutely true. But I have also met a number of adults from conventional schooling who have said that their experience of boarding at school was a real pleasure for them, and they felt that they had a wonderful childhood. More importantly, we need to consider the environment that children are living in when they are away from home.

So, is it okay for them to go to a summer camp without their parents? Is it okay to stay with friends? How about living for a while with their grandparents? When we think of it like this, then we can see that we are not in any way talking about children being wrested away from the bosom of their families and sent off to the workhouse as is often the view of boarding schools in modern society; it is more about children choosing to go to an environment that they find fulfils what they want and need in their lives. It has no reflection whatsoever upon how much they love their parents or how much the parents love them, or how happy they may be at home.

First of all, the fact that children are away from the adults they are most strongly connected with would seem to be a weakness, but actually, it is an enormous strength. They still have adults around them to love and care for them and keep them safe, but these are not the adults in the world that the children have invested in, not the people that matter the most to them in the way that their parents do.

They will not have the strong connection and sense of obligation and expectation they would have with their families. This means that the children can live their own childhood without feeling that they must fulfil some criteria from those they love. We cannot underestimate this connection and feeling of obligation that children have to their parents, even when it is absolutely not warranted or asked for.

Children crave the company of other children more than they desire to be with adults. They want to be able to play and socialise with other children to the degree that we adults cannot really grasp. If this is fulfilled, then the actual need to be with the people they love the most is not as important as we think. Provided, of course, and this is a big one, provided that they have a good loving relationship with this family and feel they can trust them and know that they will always be there for them in the background. So, to repeat what we have learned from this: Being away from the family works for the children, not in spite of the fact that they are away from those they love the most, but because of it.

Watching the children as they settle into the school, I observe a kind of lightness in them, rather as though they have taken off some heavy clothing.

Now, I do not want to suggest in any way that this is because the relationship with their parents is a negative thing. It is not, and it does not mean that parents are putting huge pressure on the children; it does not mean that there are high expectations, although obviously, it can occur in some families.

I am not recommending or expecting that people send their children to boarding school. What it means is that we generally do not recognise just how much of an inhibiting influence it can be to live with somebody who you love very dearly and with whom your whole life is firmly entwined. I see time and time again how children feel this huge responsibility towards their parents, how they try to help when things are going a bit rocky in the family. Sometimes a child will say that they wish to leave the school and live at home, which can be clearly traced to the fact that the parents are not getting along well and the child, mistakenly, feels that they need to be at home to help put things right. We need to recognise this as an expectation, not from us or from society but from the child itself.

Expectations

Many people may pass Summerhill on the road and consider that, although a brilliant idea, there must surely be things that can be improved. Of course, nothing should be beyond improvement, but if you are talking about a whole system with all of its parts interlinked and one that has been running for a hundred years using this same formula, then you have to be very careful not to pull one of the bricks out at the bottom of the pile. It is only a very tiny brick, after all, and you may not see the significance of that little brick in making up the whole thing until the rest of them come tumbling down!

A rather extreme example of this could be some of the government school inspectors who have visited us regularly. When they come, they usually find there are many things about the school that they very much like — the confidence of the pupils, their creativity, their self-motivation, their fairness and sensitivity. You can almost see the inspectors rubbing their hands together with delight. They might well be thinking: *'Now, if only we could add compulsory classes to this set-up, that would make it just about perfect'.*

Of course, they are wrong. Terribly, dangerously wrong. What makes this school work for its pupils and helps them to grow into the self-assured young people that they become is, among other things, the very fact that they *do not have to go to lessons.*

Many things may seem small and unimportant but in fact, are vital parts of the big picture. If you shaved some of those off, then you would lose part of a delicate recipe.

The relationship with the children and their feelings of ownership of the school, their particular areas, their friends, the adults, the freedom to be themselves, and the lack of judgment from the community play an essential role in allowing each person to be an individual.

Although the community will show a complete lack of judgment on individuality, expectations of behaviour are strong and well defined. Whilst nobody would bother if you dress in the conventional clothes of another sex or whether your behaviour is out of the ordinary in any way, they will certainly take a lot of notice if you behave in an unacceptable way, break the school rules, or cause anybody else discomfort or pain.

The school democratic Meetings make very few allowances when it comes to unacceptable behaviour. Though the sanctions are mild, they are fair, and if things go seriously wrong, then they can be harsh.

Summerhill children are at the school to have their own life, to quote Oliver Cromwell, 'warts and all'. They are not there for their parents or

At the end of a school day your questions can feel heavy with expectation ... perhaps look at it the other way round.

family but for themselves. This is what the parents have chosen for their children and they may make many sacrifices to ensure that this is what the children will get.

The children all know that the status quo 'out there' means going to school and learning lessons daily. They already probably feel insecure about the issue of not attending classes, just because compulsory attendance is what happens 'out there'.

Pupils at Summerhill need to come to a place where they are at peace with their learning, or the lack of it, where they feel confident with the decisions they have made about it. If they feel pressure, even benign pressure, they will react to it. They may make up little stories for themselves such as: 'Lessons are too easy', or, 'I don't know how to access the things I want' or, 'the teachers are rubbish', etc. or they may just get a bad conscience, which will impact upon their daily lives at school, making them anxious or sometimes resentful and angry.

Children in mainstream education can find the same kind of expectations from their parents. They know that they should be doing 'well' at school; they are tested and reported upon at every turn. It can become almost intolerable to some children, although they would not necessarily recognise what it is exactly that is making them anxious. They want to please their parents and friends, they want to 'keep up' with all the others, and they know the expected standard for all young people — usually imagining that everybody else is far better at it than they are. Also, of course, they are afraid of being 'different' in case they get bullied.

Very often, merely the interest that a family shows in their child's day can be a pressure. When they come home from school, it feels nice to chat to them about their day and ask how things have gone or what they were doing. It is done out of interest and is a polite and pleasant way to behave, just as we might with the other adults in our lives.

For you, as family and friends, it probably feels as though you are asking about the school day to show interest, but for your child, the questions can feel heavy with expectation. This can impact on their lives because, by implication, they think they are supposed to be doing well at lessons or enjoying school, or their dance class or football, and they actually may not be enjoying it at all.

Perhaps if you look at it the other way around — How about if your children asked you what you have been doing today? Did you get the shopping done? Did you wash that dirty kitchen floor? How many glasses of wine did you drink this evening? How much did you earn last week?

So, perhaps the next time your child comes home, whether they have been at school, out with friends or playing upstairs — You could try talking about the weather ...

In order to take something from the Summerhill model into our homes and schools, we need to find ways to create a strong sense of community and personal ownership for the children. I hate to harp on about it, but to do this, we have to find ways to let our children alone. Let us look back on our expectations and try to recognise just how much pressure we are putting upon our children without ever being aware that this is what we are actually doing.

Being emotional or sentimental about our kids is a difficult thing to shed, but we must. We must stop being so supportive, so proud, so overprotective. I know this sounds draconian, but that is absolutely not what I mean. I do not mean that we should be cold to our children, unloving or afraid to praise them — that would make me just as wrong as Truby King[1], the Victorian health reformer. What I mean is that we need to take a close look at our own emotional qualities, our own intentions and just how much of this could be about us and our feelings. We need to learn to step away and not let our own emotions cloud the issue. One of the biggest problems in our rearing of families is this inability to step away from the character that we are and give the children the benefit and respect of letting them start with a clean slate.

---

1 *Truby King — New Zealand practitioner who advocated a strict feeding regime for babies every four hours only and outlined a method that ensured that children created the minimum of disturbance to their parents' lives. He said baby and mother should 'live by the clock'. This resulted in stories of mothers sitting weeping at the bottom of the stairs. Their aching breasts were running with milk while their baby wailed with hunger and distress as they watched the clock tick slowly towards the magic four-hour time between feeds set by the Truby King regime.*

Self-government

It is not unusual for adults and children at Summerhill to make their own rules and decisions. Three times a week, the Summerhill community meets together for an hour to discuss issues, hear grievances and mete out sanctions to those who are brought up. These are known as 'fines'. From this experience, the children learn to be self-confident, tolerant and considerate, as well as become accustomed to hearing the other person's point of view.

The school Meetings are very informal but also very serious. There is no formal judiciary system or constitution, just everybody in a room together following a well-tried formula.

The self-government at Summerhill is a well-oiled machine, the same process having been in operation since the school began in 1921. Each child coming into the school joins the system and begins, from the first day, to learn the process of democracy and decision-making. This ensures that there is no sense of lawlessness or anarchy but a safe, structured environment governed by adults and children alike.

The community manages all of its everyday business such as bedtimes, wake-up times, littering laws, safety laws, etc. There are about 400 laws, probably more than in any other school: they are varied and sometimes intricate. The Meeting is also the place where children bring one another up for teasing, stealing or what is commonly called 'harassment'. There is seldom real bullying because it is brought to the public domain before it actually gets that far. There is no stigma attached to talking openly about it. Everybody in the community learns that they have a voice and a right to be heard if something is bothering them. They also learn that we speak openly and honestly about misdemeanours, and after a while, they begin to 'own up' if they are accused of doing something wrong. The crime itself may not be a huge matter, but it is better to have it talked about and not keep any guilt hanging around.

The Meeting gives the perpetrator and the victim a chance to move on, which is important to both parties.

Fines vary and often fit the crime, such as 'back of all queues' for causing problems in the lunch queue or being gated for two days for failing to use the sign-out system. If you use computers or TVs during the time when it is not allowed, then you can get a two-day screen ban.

There are many committees elected by the community to do a variety of tasks in the school. Bedtimes Officers put people to bed, get them up in the morning and maintain quiet, dishing out fines such as a screen ban or a swimming session ban if people don't follow the rules.

Ombudsmen can offer immediate help in solving problems or bring cases to the Meeting for younger or shyer pupils or non-English speakers. Only those with experience of Summerhill can do this job.

Away from Summerhill, can any of this be brought into our typical, daily lives in ordinary family homes?

We cannot have a democratic Meeting in the same sense because there are not enough people in a typical family home but also because the players will all have too close a relationship for it to be seriously workable.

I have tried to give a broad picture of how our school Meetings and self-government work, how we bring cases against one another and carry sanctions against the perpetrator in many cases to give justice to the victim and deter further unwelcome behaviour in the future. It might seem like an excellent idea to try to emulate something similar at home as this might eliminate the adult-child power conflict that can arise in a family situation. But this has its difficulties because the Meeting is not transferable to a small domestic setting; it is perhaps the *spirit* of the Summerhill process that might be the inspiration for individual families to work with here.

Personally, I would never try to punish my children or 'fine' them, even via a family Meeting. It is very different in the Summerhill Meeting and cannot be exactly replicated at home. If you fine or punish your children, then it will change your relationship with them; it will not be an even, equal one. They will get angry and, naturally, take it very personally. That is not to say that children in a family setting can do whatever they like, but any action from parents needs to be a direct result of the behaviour, not a punishment. For instance, if you need action about a particular thing such as making too much noise and disturbing the neighbours. For small children, you need to find a way of avoiding the problem altogether because, realistically, they will not be able to monitor themselves; they are just too young for that. With older ones, you can get together to talk about it and come up with various solutions such as setting times or restricting games or even talking to the neighbours to find out exactly what the problem is and how they feel it needs to be solved. Perhaps if everybody makes some compromises it can all end happily.

For more direct action such as lots of mess or noise in your house, I think the same applies. Remove the issue with little children and discuss it with older ones, or both if you have a diverse range of ages. I would probably consider little children to be those under the age of seven or so. For older children, there certainly needs to be room for discussion and compromise from both sides. Having an agreement that is understood is far more valuable than trying to be the policeman and mete out sanctions. There must be some things that all members of a family feel they can discuss and offer solutions to. I would be cautious not to try and involve the children in every decision. So long as your children feel that you have respect for them and their ideas and views, then you will find that they do not want to be involved in many of the family decisions, and so it should be. We are not trying to create little adults, just children with a feeling of control and inclusion in the way they live their lives.

The Meetings at Summerhill are needed on a regular basis because we have around 100 people in the whole community (usually 70 children 30 staff), and there will always be something to talk about and discuss. Still, in a family home, it is a bit contrived to call a regular family Meeting. Better if people are all comfortable with discussing things when and if they feel the need.

Never be afraid to be honest with your kids. Telling them about your worries or concerns is not the same thing as having expectations. You need to be up-front and straight with everybody in the family, and this can be achieved easily by being open. Make sure that what you talk about is age-appropriate. You must also be available to have your fears allayed and listening to the other point of view, which might be difficult if you have not had this kind of upbringing. Good parenting is all about looking at ourselves and our own motives and anxieties and doing our very best not to project them upon our children.

With computer gaming for instance, I would be thinking of having discussions and making my own fears quite clear — 'I am not happy with you spending all day gaming online and here are the reasons why: You are getting no exercise (reasons why you need the exercise), you are anti-social (reasons why that is not okay with me)', etc. But you need to be willing to hear the child's point of view for discussion as well.

In my experience, children are very receptive to chats like this. They really do understand where we are coming from and will go out of their way to reach a good compromise. Maybe in the school holidays, they get a week or so when they can just go crazy and spend ALL day playing, but then there will be an expectation of some sort of management. The hours we have at Summerhill work very well. No screens before 4 pm or after bedtime, except at weekends when there are only limits at bedtime. This is obviously just a loose suggestion, but it gives an idea of how things can work out in a family home.

Equality

'What strikes you immediately, coming from the world outside and talking to the kids at Summerhill, is that you can't tell the boys from the girls. This is important. It's not just hairstyles and jeans. The girls are so self-reliant and the boys so concerned, the girls so calmly tough and the boys so gentle. No boy's voice has that conditioned flick of off-handedness that says, "I am male". They are interested voices, friendly and lightly generous, and their bodies are not tautly aggressive but trusting. You are startled when you hear their names. You begin to wonder how early children are warped in the world outside, dumped straight from the cradle onto one side of the line they must never step over, separated from one another and from their complete selves, permanently angered. Neill once said at a progressive school conference, listening to them talk about how to keep the boys from the girls and pressed for his opinion, "Why don't you put up barbed wire?" '
Quotation by Leila Berg from Neill & Summerhill, a Man and his Work, by John Walmsley. Penguin Books 1969.

Society is trying to create gender equality for all the right reasons but is going about it in entirely the wrong way. We are putting a sticking plaster on the problem instead of solving the problem itself. Stopping little girls from listening to stories about princesses being kissed by handsome princes is one such extreme sticking plaster. Trying to change the names of things to make them sound less about 'man' is another. Fisherwoman, firewoman, by all means change those names but do not expect that it will make society fairer or produce more strong, confident women because it will not.

A well-known lady MP, Barbara Castle, once said: *'I don't care if you call me the Chairwoman, the Chairperson or the Chairman — so long as I am in the chair.'* That just about sums it up — brilliant! Because no matter how many times you tell somebody that they are strong, equal, and just as good as everybody else, there is not likely to be much progress at all unless they really feel it.

This is not just about gender equality; it is about how children of all types, denominations, sexes and colours feel about themselves, their own confidence and their self-esteem. Not allowing boys to be gentle people who are caring and perceptive is something that has been discriminating against men for centuries. 'Boys don't cry, take it like a man!' We have all heard those things, and it is disgraceful and a slur upon our society that we are still letting it happen.

Boys don't cry — take it like a man.
Not allowing boys or men to be gentle, caring and perceptive is disgraceful,
and a slur on society.

Recently I watched a six-year-old girl bring a case to our Summerhill School democratic Meeting. In a room full of around 60 people, most of them much bigger than she, this little girl put up her hand to ask for a case and then sat quietly waiting.

When the Chair called her, she confidently brought up another girl who had screamed into the ear of her five-year-old friend and made her friend cry. The case was briefly discussed, the sanction voted upon, the perpetrator getting a 'Strong Warning' not to bully.

This little girl already knows that she is as good as anybody, that her case will be heard, that she is valuable in her community and has the same rights as anybody else. This is not a precocious little Madam used to getting her own way but a sweet, calm, strong, young person who sometimes wears pink frilly girlie clothes and, yes, sometimes watches movies about princesses.

Vitally, this is all about children learning to trust and value themselves, knowing their true worth as people, not as a particular race or gender, but as strong individuals with their emotions open and unrepressed.

Living in an environment where everybody has equal status and honesty and open emotions are the everyday norm, pupils naturally acquire a high degree of emotional intelligence, which is increasingly sought after in many work environments. They leave the school with outstanding personal skills and the ability to communicate, negotiate and compromise — three essential basics needed in life, whatever the road that is taken. As well as this, Summerhill pupils develop, through living in the community as they do, a powerful sense of understanding and compassion for the problems of others.

As Leila Berg states, the boys are gentle souls, caring of the women around them and open in their emotions. When the Department for Education sent a group of Inspectors to see if Summerhill children were harmed by living in mixed-sex corridors (against the rules in UK schools), we asked a group of our former students who had recently graduated and gone on to college to talk to them about their own experiences of living closely with the opposite sex. All agreed that this had been an amazingly strong and positive influence on them in the way they feel and behave. Sadly, one of the first things that came up was how the boys, now attending two separate colleges, were finding terrible bias and basic sexism from their new, otherwise very nice, male friends. They were shocked by the level of discrimination there was from the boys toward the girls around them, the aggressive jokes, the obscenities and their general attitudes.

Funny, we talk about all sorts of discrimination against groups in our society, but we never look at the terrible way that boys have for centuries been repressed and indoctrinated to step away from their natural feelings of compassion and tenderness in order to be hard.

The idea has been to control their feelings and treat women with disrespect and often contempt. This has taken a tremendous toll on the emotions of boys and men — and now they seem to be getting all the blame for the attitude which societies and child-rearing have thrust upon them.

I am not suggesting that our teenagers should be squeaky clean — there will always be a bit of ribaldry between the sexes, always be a bit of teasing or suggestiveness. So long as this is equal, fun and not bullying anybody, then it is really part of growing into a sexually aware adult.

Summerhill's thrice-weekly Meetings enable them to understand the importance of themselves as individuals and how their involvement can impact on the whole school community.

We are trying to make sure that we are giving children the respect that we would give other people and through this their self-confidence and therefore their feeling of equality will grow. As parents, you don't have to worry about princesses being kissed by handsome princes or young heroes being hard and macho; generations of strong women and the gentlest of men have been reared watching Cinderella and Superman, and it did not affect them negatively at all, provided that they were in homes where their own role-models were showing strength, compassion, leadership, kindness and love.

The adults in the Summerhill community are, of course, in a caring role and take the responsibility very seriously — but they work hard to ensure that it doesn't affect the equality in their relationships with the pupils. It is this real equality that assists the pupils in the development of their self-confidence and feeling of self-worth.

How are we going to bring this equality into our homes? I believe that the first step we can take towards this is treating our children with respect and honesty — the kind of respect that we would expect from another adult. We must have very high standards in how we address our children and how we behave with our children whilst always understanding that children are children and we should not ask for more than their age and ability. Our interactions should be playful, fun and warm-hearted, sometimes kindly teasing or being teased, but serious when it is needed. We need to be aware of the limits of a young child's perception and understanding and try to fashion their freedom around this.

Even Summerhill children can be obnoxious at times (or did I give the impression that they are always wonderful saints?). They make a mess, they argue and can be generally unpleasant to live with, especially after bedtime when they are creeping around (like a herd of elephants) and keeping you awake.

I am a realist. I do not live in cloud cuckoo land. I know that we adults sometimes lose the plot and shout in anger at our children. It is important to accept what we have done and take it on the chin. None of us is superhuman, and looking after little children can sometimes push us over the edge. Accept what you did, feel bad about it too if you like, but always make sure that you will never cross the line and bully or intimidate no matter how angry you are. Children usually see plain honest anger for what it is unless they have been intimidated and frightened by an adult in the past — and that is not within the remit of this book.

We must ensure that children feel in control of their own lives by respecting their views, allowing them to disagree with us, and letting them have choices in their lives and some control. Always remember that you need to talk to your child with the restraint and respect you would show to your best friend, and we often have differences of opinion with our friends, don't we? By all means get a bit annoyed with them but keep it as respectful as you can. You need to step out of the usual way adults talk to children, which if you analyse it and watch it being played out in front of you, most often means talking down to them or, equally bad, being patronisingly 'nice'.

I have an example of a new girl we had at school. She was a bit what we would call 'indulged' at home. She was used to playing up to the grown-ups by saying pert, affected things to get their attention and impress them. This girl was about nine years old. She came up to me often in her early weeks and 'presented herself' in front of me as a bit of a Ta-Da moment. After a while, I had to respectfully tell her that I was not impressed with that kind of behaviour, that I would rather she was just herself and could come up and have a pleasant, normal conversation with me. I think I shocked her but I did make a real effort not to humiliate her. She soon stopped putting on that act and we had many more normal, friendly chats together from then on.

I know a lot of grown-ups who would have thought I was completely out of order to say what I did, but I did not frighten or humiliate the girl and the truth was that she really annoyed me with that infantile behaviour, so I felt it was the right thing to do to tell her.

Some Summerhill parents naturally find it very difficult when their children call home and say that things are not going well. It might be that they want to come home, that the food is rubbish, that they are having a hard time with their friends. Sometimes this builds up to a regular feature that the family perceive as home-sickness. We always tell parents to contact us as we see how the child is faring in their daily life.

When we have established that all is well, I usually advise parents to confront the child because it is upsetting to have phone calls every day saying how sad they are. This is not all about you — the child — it is about us, your family as well. How do you think I feel if you keep moaning and crying all the time? We made this decision to have you at Summerhill, and you were in favour of it too because you were not happy where you were in the previous school. So, let us decide: if you want to come home and go back to your old school with all of its problems then let us do that, but if you're going to stay at Summerhill then for goodness' sake just get on with it, take control of your life and stop moaning about it to us.

Now, I know that many people will throw their hands up in disgust at this, but if we are talking about equality, then sometimes things like this need to be said. The problem is that most parents feel they need to 'be there' for their children, that they must always be sympathetic and kind. Sometimes you need to say what has to be said, even if it seems a bit harsh.

At home these circumstances will apply many times as well. We, as parents, become very accustomed to absorbing a lot of moaning and misery from our children when things are not quite perfect. I strongly believe that in an equal relationship with our children there has to be room for the parents to have a bit of understanding and respect as well. It goes without saying that this will all be age-appropriate. A crying five-year-old will need a different reaction from parents compared with a 12-year-old. However, even a five-year-old can get the simple version in a clearly explained way — basically, life cannot be all about you all the time, I am a human being and my well-being is important too.

Another story about equality shows that even I can be surprised by the way I perceive small children. I was watching a little girl of five as we stood in the lunch queue at Summerhill. There was a group of older boys there, aged about 14 to 16. They were being rowdy and loud, shoving each other a bit but not so much that it bothered me (I would have told them to stop if it had). However, I was keeping an eye on the little girl and a bit worried that she might find the situation intimidating as they had loud voices and were so huge compared to her. She just stood there quietly. We reached the front of the queue; the boys were in front and duly took their food into the dining room and sat down at a table to eat. The little girl followed with me behind.

When I got into the dining room, I was just in time to see this tiny girl, with all the confidence in the world, collect her knife and fork, look around the room for a place to sit and then make a beeline for the table with the big rowdy boys. I was amazed, surprised and delighted in equal measure. How I had misjudged or made assumptions about the way the girl viewed these big, loutish teenage boys. She clearly thought of them as safe to be around, and she wanted to enjoy her lunch in their company. What a delight! It just shows how we need to constantly refresh our own views and assumptions about our children and the way they think about things.

Freedom

Message to children everywhere — *'Make sure that your parents are busy living their own lives'* — that way you will be free to enjoy more of life's challenges for yourself.

We have to be prepared to think outside the box on this one. Giving children freedom means 'freedom from' as much, if not much more, than 'freedom to'. It is quite a complex thing and may mean really sitting down and deciding what this freedom means to you and your views on child-rearing and how it might work for your family.

In a nutshell, when most children finish their mainstream education, perhaps when they move out to go to college or university, they are actually very unprepared for the decision making that will be part of their lives from that point on. This is not surmising; it is a fact. In conventional education and in many homes, children are not part of the decision-making process and do not have a forum to practice decision-making.

Making decisions, like everything else, is something that you get better at the more you practice. I am sure that we all shudder at some of the mistakes we have made in our own lives!

A good guideline to freedom in everyday home life should be: **Will it break anything, upset anybody, be dangerous (really dangerous — not imagined), or will it drive you up the wall?** If it does not fit these criteria, then 'Cry havoc and let slip the dogs of war'. Stand back and enjoy it. Sometimes things that we think would not be okay actually turn out to be a huge success, and sometimes it is the other way around when we might need to step in pretty forcefully to make sure that it ends fast before something else goes wrong.

We have an area at Summerhill called the Clay Hump. It is at the bottom of a slope by the school office, mainly used for cycling down or riding on crazy homemade sledge contraptions. Sometimes after a heavy rain, this pit fills quite quickly with water to a depth of around 60 centimetres. From time to time, a group of younger kids will start to paddle in the new pool and play by making boats out of all sorts of old, unwanted stuff and generally just having a wonderful time. It never takes long before somebody falls over and gets soaked. This is the sign for the others to wade in, get fiendishly muddy or even strip off their clothes and go in naked. We are talking about children from about five to 11 years old. One's first reaction is to look at the mud, look at the mess, look at the shivering children and flinch. But then you look at the delight, the joy and the sense of real freedom those children are feeling because nobody is telling them to keep out of the water; in fact, nobody is telling them what to do at all, and you can see that no matter how wet and muddy they might get, it is all worth it.

When the game is over, there will be time for a tidy up, and I doubt that anybody is going to be allowed to walk into the main house in that state, so it should not be a trouble to anybody indoors. They can be thrown a towel and some dry clothes in the porch and threatened with dire consequences if they set foot on the carpet! Nothing broken, nobody hurt (apart from probably being freezing cold), and washing machines do a great job these days.

There is a lot remarked upon in the media these days about children needing to spend good 'family' time with their family. I think we should be a bit careful of this as it implies in an oblique way that only time spent with the family can be a good time.

It is very important for children to have time with their families but let us not underestimate the importance of kids having time without parents or other adults around. They need an awful lot of this, much more than we adults like to think they need. It is through this time spent with other children that they are learning the truly valuable lessons about interacting with others, about living with one's fellows, about being an individual and about taking responsibility, however small, for one's actions.

Although I am advocating the need for children to spend time on their own, I am also saying that children sometimes cannot work out their differences entirely without the help and input of an adult or older child, hence at Summerhill, our system of Ombudsmen. No play ever goes completely smoothly. It is the very nature of young children to argue and bicker — this is how they learn about how to get along with one another. There will be many mistakes and much arguing before they emerge as butterflies!

Children are only truly able to be uninhibited when playing among their peers, for it is only then that they feel completely free of any kind of expectations. We need to learn to be the adult that can fade into the background so that the children will play in that free and unconscious way. It is a great skill and worth working hard to achieve. Probably the very best way is to ensure that you are busy and engaged in your own

*Adults need to fade into the background, so that children can play
in a free and unconscious way.*

work or interests whilst being able to keep a weather eye upon the proceedings. Reading is a good one as it keeps you entertained without actually being in the room so-to-speak. If you watch TV or a film, it might draw the children in to join you and thereby spoil the moment.

Many wonderful new enterprises are springing up where children can go and do fun things in the forest — building dens, playing with water and mud, finding fungi. It is great to see them being used and appreciated — BUT — if only they would have a separate campfire for the parents to sit by, to talk about grown-up things, have a coffee and ignore what the kids are doing. It would transform the experience from a very good one to a truly wonderful one. Used on a regular basis it could even start its own little self-government meetings …

To illustrate the lack of status we ought to have, A. S. Neill famously told a story about a new boy at Summerhill who wrote home to his mother halfway through his first term saying: 'There is a chap here called Neill, I like him'. It tells us a lot about Neill and his status as an adult. He was the Headmaster and the boy did not know it! I feel that many headteachers, even of modern schools, might not like that very much.

My own story is of a nine-year-old boy who has been at Summerhill for at least two years. He often comes running up and asks if he can have my tea biscuits. I 'hum' and 'ha' for a few moments, deciding if I want them for myself, and then I say 'Yes' and he can have them.

He says: 'Yay! Thanks', and turns to run off. Then he stops, turns around and looks serious for a moment.

He asks: 'Who ARE you?'

Well, that puts me firmly in my place!

Freedom 'to' and freedom 'from'

When we talk of freedom, it is always associated with the ability to do something and this applies strongly to the idea of freedom for children. One of the things that has dogged Summerhill for most of its life is the idea that freedom for children means total anarchy with wild 'Lord of the Flies' children running around setting light to buildings just for fun. Summerhill freedom is nothing like that. We have already talked about freedom with responsibility, and the fact that the school has about 400 laws which we are all, adults and pupils, expected to observe.

Let us look at freedom 'from' and exactly what it means.

One thing I see an awful lot of is the result of parental or perceived parental expectation. Expectation is one of those things that few parents would admit to; in fact, most would vehemently deny it. But it is a cunning little devil that pops its head up in the most surprising disguises and in families where you would not expect to find it.

Traditionally I suppose expectation would be thought of in a very Victorian way. The family that makes it clear to their children exactly what they are 'supposed' to do with their lives, what qualifications they should gain, which degree, and finally, what career they should take up as an adult. 'We expect you to get a good degree, young man, and then it is into the bank like your father'.

But no, expectation is much deeper than that, much more subtle. It can come from the most well-meaning parents whose only motivation is the love of their children. It need not be about qualifications; it can just be living in a family where everybody else is a 'high achiever'. Maybe professional parents with good degrees, maybe a musical family, maybe siblings who have 'done well for themselves'. It can come from parents who engage a lot with their children, play with them, talk to them, spend a lot of time with them. The unsaid can often be more of an expectation than the said.

Nobody is even likely to notice it at the time, but I have seen many children over the years who become very anxious or have low self-esteem; when we get talking, it transpires that the child has felt pressured, sometimes almost pressured by love and approval. Perhaps the pressure has come from the children themselves wanting to be the very best that they can be to live up to some perceived ambition which, in fact, does not exist. At home, we need to be watchful of this and be ready to explain our own lack of aspirations for our children — except that we wish them as much happiness as life can offer them.

I keep mentioning this external or internal pressure only because, almost without exception, every child who comes to Summerhill simply cannot wait to be a boarder, away from the family they dearly love. This is not just a chance coincidence. Children from all backgrounds, countries, and families will almost all simply crave it. And the number of emails I get from all over the world reinforces what I am saying. Children begging to be allowed to come and live at Summerhill, not to get away from the family they hate but to get away from the family they most dearly love.

So, coming back to individual families, how to give them that independence and lack of encumbrance in our own homes and schools? It is a difficult one to tackle.

Are you competitive? Do you constantly praise your child when they win or do well in a project? Or do you bring a lot of humour into the family games, make a bit of a chump of yourself, let yourself be seen as a happy loser or a joyous ignoramus who cannot possibly understand what the child understands? This can be a great way to lower the feeling of expectation. Humour always wins in my view and a parent prepared to make a bit of a fool of themselves is often streets ahead.

Of course, young children need praise, but not for every little thing that they do. Once again, it is for you to look at yourself and make these decisions about how much pressure you might be putting on without actually meaning to at all.

Sometimes we need to look at our children and recognise that they are not perfect little people, that they actually do like too much sugar, that they do like too much TV and that, yes, they may well start smoking later in their teenage years — even though it is abhorrent to you (and to me too actually). Only if we can see this reality can we take steps to address it in a good old common-sense way.

A. S. Neill wrote:
'It must be emphasised again and again that freedom does not involve spoiling a child. If a baby of three wants to walk over the table, you simply tell him he must not.'

I believe we should always be honest with our children, tell them how we feel about things, but always bear in mind that this must be age-appropriate and of interest to them, that it must not frighten or confuse them or be too personal. We should not be talking about our own issues or our marriage, or our partner. We should not be talking about the bank foreclosing on our business as this will frighten children. We have had parents at Summerhill who have stepped into that area, mistakenly thinking that being honest means telling ALL. It has caused huge problems for both them and their children. Remember, our children need to know who is in charge here and that the household and family are safe. They need to feel secure and this means knowing that even if our living partnership is breaking down, all will be sorted out amicably and gently and that they, the children, will have a voice in the resulting actions and will not be forgotten.

Having given your child as much information as you can about a subject, then you need to give them the respect of being allowed to make decisions for themselves. Do not be afraid to tell them how you feel, your own fears and concerns. Keep it honest and about the subject that you are discussing.

Spending a lot of time with children, going to the theatre, looking at landscapes or cityscapes, visiting art galleries, taking them to ballet or sports when they might not be one hundred per cent enthusiastic, all this can create a feeling of expectation on the child to perform or to be interested or to want to know more. It is always worth double-checking that they really are engaged. This is not an easy one as they will always want to please you. You may have to become a bit of an emotional detective! Look at your children, but also keep on looking at yourself. Am I doing this for them or am I doing it for me? If you are not sure, then maybe let it drop for a while and see if your child genuinely asks you if they can do it again. If you suspect that they might be going along with it to enjoy your company, then maybe try going for some companionable walks or cycle rides instead.

First of all, remember that children want approval; we all do. So, if a child feels instinctively that you would like them to be better at or be more interested in something, then they will do their best to comply. It may be that they feel they want the approval or praise, or they may just feel that they need to do this. And they may very well be mistaken about your intentions and desires in this area. Just keep in mind that if they are mistaken, then there is something that you are doing which is suggesting it to them in the first place, so you may want to look again at yourself and your mannerisms in a bit of a critical way.

It is worth keeping in mind that by the time your child is a mid-teenager, they will probably not want to do anything even remotely connected with you as an adult, so try not to be offended or hurt!

A young child at Summerhill who was very new to us was constantly telling his parents that he could not get the classes that he wanted, that they were too infantile and boring for him and that the teacher did not teach well. His parents fed back to us and were clearly very worried about it. We said that we thought he needed time to be a child and do some silliness and playing, and we felt sure that later he would settle into classwork. His parents said that we did not understand him, that he wanted to work and that he was much more mature than the other children of his age.

What our teachers were seeing was a child who loved doing craftwork and art. He enjoyed those classes that he was doing. As the time for his parents to visit got closer, he started to ask the teachers for more written work that he could send home to them to see.

After a while, it became clear that this family would not be compatible with the school ethos and, sure enough, they took him out at the end of the next term.

From time to time, a child will want to leave Summerhill in order to go to a school where they have to work because they feel the need to learn and cannot create enough self-motivation to fulfil their own expectations. Of course, in time this self-motivation would arise on its own, but they may not have the patience, trust or knowledge of our system to take that time. If moving will fulfil their needs, then it is quite obviously the right thing for them to do.

Freedom 'from' brings to mind the story of a boy we had some years ago who was clearly traumatised by his life at a previous school. Unable to take full part in the classes because he could not fully understand and thus became bored, he came to us as a very anxious child with a lot of paperwork. He was determined not to take part in anything that we offered. Although polite to the adults, he was very clear that he was absolutely not interested in anything we might suggest or say. He was a day pupil, coming in at nine and leaving at 5 pm. His first two terms were quite lonely, spending many hours on his own cycling around the school grounds. He did a lot of looking at what was going on with the other children but did not join in much. When approached, he said very pointedly that he was 'fine'. So, we took his word for it, left him alone and just passed the time of day with him but otherwise pretty well left him to himself.

It was wonderful to watch the way he just left his old life behind him, sort of cycled and played his way away from it, leaving it in the past. He was not openly rebellious or angry but made it clear that once he knew that he could do whatever HE wanted at Summerhill, then he was damn sure that this was what he was going to do!

This boy was closely monitored and discussed regularly in staff meetings to ensure that, although we were giving him space to learn to be at peace with himself, we were also anxious to ensure that there was plenty on offer. Although we try to allow the pupils at Summerhill to live their own lives and not to rely upon us adults for entertainment, in this case, we were happy to be more hands-on and to offer rather more leadership just to help this little chap with his transition. So various staff offered him the things that he enjoyed and that he could help with without too many other people being involved. He did some gardening with a keen gardener on the staff and some other outdoor things, and gradually he became more integrated.

As always, it was a real joy to see a child growing and gaining so much confidence. Some people might argue that we were not preparing this boy for his future life because he was not learning in class. But we argue strongly that he was in a far better position to meet the challenges of life ahead of him without the inhibitions and fears that he was storing up and the reams of paperwork that would follow him. He was a free agent, an autonomous human being who was already learning about taking responsibility for himself and, eventually, for those around him.

He will probably always be an honest individual with his own set of rules about life — but he learned the all-important lesson, that we all have to fit in with other people in some way or the other, become team players to some degree and that there are certain expectations of each of us in the way we socially interact with others; but that is all — no need to go to class and do things that frighten you. This newfound confidence enabled him to enjoy many things that would not have been available to him before. It is always lovely to see him when he visits and he still always sends me a Christmas card.

Choosing to go barefoot in November is a personal freedom —
it doesn't impact on others. Nobody should force you to wear shoes.

Personal freedom vs licence
'Barefoot in November'

A. S. Neill wrote:

'You cannot have freedom unless children feel completely free to govern their own social life.'

There is a lot of confusion about what personal freedom really is. I was watching a boy of 15 walking outside on a cold November morning without any shoes on. It suddenly dawned on me that this simple action perfectly sums up what personal freedom and the freedom at Summerhill means. Personal freedom is actually a simple thing. It is your right to please yourself, provided that this does not impact upon somebody else. So if you do not want to wear shoes on a cold November morning — nobody should be able to make you do so.

I would, however, add a rider to this — later in the January, at Summerhill, we had a lot of snow and ice. Many of the younger children were walking around barefoot, a little craze they had all been following since the previous summer. It is clearly not all right for young children to play in the snow with no shoes on, so our school Meeting made a rule that nobody could go barefoot for the remainder of the winter term (January-April). I think this is a very clear illustration of Summerhill School democracy in action, of the difference between freedom and licence and the fact that young children do need direction and sympathetic but firm guidance.

What I see a lot of in life all over the age spectrum is a yearning to do exactly as we want. We see it in all walks of life, certainly in the Western world anyway. Older people often have a 'Bucket List' of things that they want to do. It seems that the pursuit of happiness has become the prime interest in life. My concern is that this word 'happiness' is a very loaded one. What is happiness? Who can define it? My happiness need not be your happiness, so how can we agree on what the word means? Perhaps pursuing happiness is a sign of the relatively physically indolent world that many of us live in. I am guessing that our ancient ancestors had little time to even think about happiness as they were too busy surviving!

Sadly, for many people, the word 'happiness' means a life of no worry, of no strife, very often of no responsibility. It means a complete indulgence in what 'I' want with little regard for how it may impact on other people or the planet. In a broad sense, we see this daily with many abuses of nature, mostly just because we want to enjoy things easily and comfortably. We also see a massive divide between what we in the West would regard as 'happiness' and what others less fortunate than ourselves would consider to be happiness.

People often mistake 'wanting their own way' with personal freedom. This is a dangerous quest. None of us can have everything that we want. We cannot behave the way we want at all times. Life is not like that. I think that giving anybody, particularly children, the idea that this is something they can achieve is terrible.

Sometimes young teenagers, in their quest to get their own way, which they often sell to themselves and those around them as their right to a 'free spirit', can become resentful and angry when society will not go along with their wishes. This soon becomes a fight against authority or any perceived authority.

In Summerhill, there is only the school Meeting to rebel against, but that will often suffice. It can take quite a time for a child to realise that 'getting your own way' is quite an infantile concept — they can feel as though everybody is against them and that they are being victimised. This in itself is a strong reason for children to learn right from the start what personal freedom really is. It is something that all parents can do at home, right from the very beginning. None of us is free to do exactly as we like, and we all need to be aware of this fact to move forward and get settled into a satisfying life.

It is very easy for parents to mistake freedom for licence. Due to their passionate love for their children, they allow this love to overwhelm the relationship. In other words, they give so much love, care and approval that the child ends up being, in old-fashioned terms, a bit spoilt. The child becomes accustomed to getting what they want when they want it. Their parents might very well not see that this is the case and would probably deny it vigorously. This is why I suggest constantly reassessing what we are doing in our homes, checking out to make sure that we are not falling into this trap in particular. It is hard to stand back and take a cool, calculated look, but we really need to do this from time to time. We need our love and leadership to be unsentimental, and we need to be able, when it is necessary, to just say that most simple of words in a strong and assertive way: 'NO!'

A child who has called most of the shots for all of their lives will find it very difficult to give that up — if they ever really can. Often children like this can become little tyrants in their own homes.

One father told me that they had never had to say 'No' to their son because they always discussed issues in a grown-up fashion and reached a unanimous agreement. From our observations of the boy, we at

Summerhill concluded that a 'unanimous agreement' meant that the boy had almost always got exactly what he wanted!

He was a complete pain to the community and his peer group for many years until around the age of fourteen, and after many school Meeting hours spent bringing cases against him, he settled down. But he remained rebellious to many community decisions under the guise of being a 'free spirit'. I don't see how his early rearing had been helpful to him at all. Without our school system at Summerhill with the Ombudsmen and Meetings, I think he would have grown into a very selfish person with little insight into the needs of others or any idea at all of the fact that people sometimes have to learn to toe-the-line whether they like it or not.

Interestingly, this boy was a very kind soul, which came to the fore as he grew older. He became quite a solid 'big kid' in the school and was thoughtful in discussing the younger one's cases in the school Meeting, becoming a bit of a village 'elder' — and much respected.

A while back, we had a young boy of five who only came in as a day pupil, not a boarder. His home was nearby the school and one day he went home to collect something he had forgotten. He was brought up in the school Meeting and his sanction was not to be allowed to come to school until lunchtime the following day. He loved it at school and was somewhat stroppy about this, having a bit of a tantrum and sulking, but the community in the Meeting made it clear that he would have to observe this fine, which he did. He never went home out of hours again. In fact, after a couple of terms of having various fines, he became a different citizen altogether — he was sociable, played much better with his peers and seldom if ever, got brought up in the Meetings. He was also swift to offer advice in a mature and helpful fashion if he thought there had been an injustice.

I know that it is different at Summerhill because we are a large community and we have Meeting structures in place, but I use this as an illustration that being a bit hard on somebody who is continually thinking only of themselves is justified, and it can also bring huge benefits.

In a Summerhill Meeting you will hear someone say that they are angry because they could not sleep last night due to the noise on the top corridor. They will propose an appropriate fine and the people involved will get fined, or a warning, or whatever. What they will not do is talk about why they are angry. They will most likely say: 'It is not right to keep people awake, you should be more thoughtful of others, you are being selfish and thoughtless, etc.' The fact is, you made a noise that is not okay, and you know it (children aren't stupid!).

Play

I hope that elsewhere I have demonstrated that Summerhill is a school; it is a successful educational learning environment where the vast majority of children go to many of the lessons at some time. But this section is headed 'Play', and it is essential to unpack 'play' and look at its length, width and depth — and, of course, its fundamental importance to the philosophy of the school and the lifestyle connected to it.

Sadly, the activity of children playing seems to be increasingly threatened and reduced in present-day civilised societies; recent research shows young children in the UK today are not allowed to go outside to play on their own until two years older than when their parents' generation did the same (British Children's Play Survey, 2021).

After a lifetime at Summerhill, I am amazed by the capacity of little children to play and play and play. It is almost non-stop from the time they get up in the morning until the time they go to bed at night. No wonder they run out of steam from time to time and get irritable or feel a bit unwell. I remember my own children returning from school in the holidays and spending the first week or so just wanting to watch TV or play computer games. You could see their young bodies and minds relaxing and restoring. It wasn't long before they were out playing again and waiting for the start of the new term. When they were very little, I noticed that around midday, they would start getting argumentative with one another, a bit fractious. This was the time to start shovelling food into their little beaks and encourage them to sit and watch a bit of TV or do something quiet. After a short while of rest, with tummies full, they were soon off again and playing.

What this shows us in the most glaring way is that for young human animals, play is their default setting. Watching them in a free-range environment, you realise how incredibly destructive are the regimes of most schools and child-rearing systems where children are required to sit still and be engaged in things that they have not actually chosen to do at all and which often challenge their abilities to the degree that causes both stress and insecurity — and often failure. Some will conform and find it relatively easy, but many more do not. It is not surprising that some children may find a voice and become defiant, which then identifies them as 'trouble makers.' This might end up being something that will take them to the educational psychologist and the diagnosis of a problem.

Discovering that a child is on the autistic spectrum, for instance, means that most schools will offer specific allowances for their particular needs and behaviours. I would argue that schools should be making these allowances to a child's individuality anyway, without any diagnosis.

Oh, if only there could be areas in schools where children who were finding it hard to sit in class could just get up and run about and play or find other things to do such as dance, woodwork, art or fun sports. I bet a million pounds that it would make every school a happier and more comfortable environment for children and teachers alike; a simple solution that would not even be too expensive to set-up and run. It must be so soul-destroying for teachers to be trying to teach some children who have absolutely no interest in what they are doing or are finding it hard to understand the concept of what they are being taught. There are some subjects that I would find mind-numbing and I can imagine that I would certainly be out to cause trouble, if only through desperation and boredom.

Some children are severely affected by some conditions, some less so. Even if children at Summerhill do not come with a diagnosis, it is straightforward to see who is affected and by what. However, this does not need a diagnosis to aid the child because that is what we do anyway, with each child as an individual. At Summerhill, we rejoice in human individuality and treasure each person's strengths and weaknesses, no matter how annoying they may be at times!

Henry David Thoreau wrote:
'If a man cannot keep up with his companions, perhaps it is because he hears a different drummer. Let him step to the rhythm he hears, however measured or far away ...'

Arrive on any day at Summerhill and the first thing you will see are children playing. Spontaneous wonderful play. They play indoors, they play outside, they play the right way up and they play upside-down. Some games are sensible and seem to have a point, and some are totally silly in every way. Playing is what Summerhill children do, like the kittens tumbling out of the box.

And when you tell a visiting child the basics of Summerhill, the very first thing they say is 'You mean I don't I have to go to lessons?' And then they run off and start playing.

Watching them, free-range children, doing what children are supposed to do, is one of those epiphanic moments in your life. The capacity for this play and the need for the company of other children is amazing. How on earth do children in conventional situations ever manage to control this all-pervading, powerful urge?

Societies worldwide do not respect children's inherent ability and desire to play. Children are hard-wired to play most of the time and we need to allow them to fulfil this need, just as we allow them to eat, breathe and sleep.

At Summerhill, play belongs to the child. We do not dress up learning situations so that the play will be 'productive'; we do not look on and evaluate what they might learn from this or that game. Our children just play — and they can do it pretty well all day if they want to.

Naturally, sometimes things go wrong during play sessions. Sometimes people get into conflict. This is part of being a child. There are structures in place that protect the rights of each of us. Big kids or adults can help out if it is needed. Even young children are encouraged to deal with some of it for themselves. There cannot always be a 'Nanny' to look after us and solve our problems in life.

Sometimes play can lead to other interests. You might start off by making a sword in the woodwork and then decide that you want to make something more. You may mess around on the old school piano and then find that you want to make music. You might join up to the Class One shop and find that you want to learn more about Maths, or make a big bang in the Science lab and then sign up for Biology. There are so many areas for inspiration and enjoyment.

Whichever way you look at it, at Summerhill play means play and it belongs entirely to you, the child.

So once again, how can we utilise this in our homes and families? Children have this tremendous capacity for play which we adults in society often do not give the recognition that it deserves. We do not seem to understand that young children, allowed to play freely with few constraints upon that play, will get up at seven in the morning and play all day long, often to the point of becoming overtired and grouchy! It is sometimes only when you can watch 'free-range' children in action on a daily basis that you realise how cruel it is to sit them down and make them listen to things that do not interest them when their hearts and minds are somewhere else.

Obviously, if your child is going to a conventional school, it can be difficult to deal with this. They are in a system that demands more time in a classroom than free play outside. Parents will need to be creative about the way they manage it. Working at home to create as much time and space for play outside of school hours is essential, perhaps re-evaluating what is actually happening in your home in the way of expectations on your child. Do they really need to go to ballet, roller skating, Karate? Is this something they really want, or do they do it

Children are hard-wired to play most of the time and we should to let them fulfil this need.

because it seemed a good idea at the time and has now become part of the weekly routine, or perhaps it is a way to see friends outside of the school environment? How about getting together with some other families and arranging some 'free play' hours when the children can be left to themselves, just to do the silly things that children often do?

If a child wants to do organised activities, it might be worth looking to see if they really do, or is it just a better alternative to staying home and doing homework? If there was a choice between Karate and just loafing around playing — which one would they choose?

Of course, they have to go to school, and there may be nothing you can do other than look for a school where the emphasis is not too strong on the academic work ethic and where there may be more in the way of sports and games or more creative things. Personally, I feel so strongly about creative play that I would take my child out of a school that was putting too much pressure on them. In other words, I might be looking at the schools in the area that were lower on the league tables instead of, like most parents, looking for the highest!

You can manage to let children have a lot of real play at home. They can spend time at the end of the garden or in the park, come in and get a sandwich and then go out again or whatever it is they want to do. Try to find ways where they can play alone, without your help. If you have to go out to find a play area, then maybe take a book and have a bit of 'me' time while they enjoy their freedom. They need to know that you are not going to appear and intrude into their playing space so that they can feel in control of it and of what they are doing. Get on with things that you need to do so they don't feel 'watched' and try to rejoice in this.

My view on play is that it is the most vital part of a child's life. If you are also a bit of a naturalist, as I am, you can see this pattern in every mammal species as they learn through their play how to use their skills for survival. That is precisely what our children are doing, honing their skills for their social interactions and survival — learning how to be humans, how to interact, how to live with one another. Through the enjoyment and rough and tumble of play, they learn the most vital components in life — communication, negotiation and compromise.

All the school subjects in the world cannot teach you to be a better human being. They can make you knowledgeable and make you rich and admired, but they cannot teach you the fundamental elements of being a caring, compassionate person.

Calm energy

This question of energy is a critical one. I will try to illustrate what I am getting at by using an example that I saw the other day on a television programme about training troublesome dogs.

There is a trainer who goes into people's houses and assists them with 'doggy' problems. This couple had a terrier that was very, very anxious. The anxiety would have come mainly from the owner's lack of expertise in caring for a dog, but that is not what is important. We are not apportioning blame or pointing fingers. The anxiety made the dog unhappy and it made the family unhappy. They were not able to take the dog out for an enjoyable walk and could not take their daughter out for the day or on holiday because of all the problems that the dog created due to his anxiety.

Watching the programme, you could very clearly see what was going wrong. Every time the family took the dog out, they would try to reassure him by telling him that he was a good boy, picking him up sometimes and constantly talking to him, thinking that they were giving him courage and strength with their sympathy and support. They were anxious themselves because of the stress of the situation (it had been going on for a few years), and you could read this in every movement in their body and their voices. They thought they were doing the right thing and reassuring the poor dog by giving him love and comforting words. But it had the opposite effect. By showing their anxiety and constantly trying to reassure the dog, they were, in fact, unwittingly sharing their own fears, which frightened the dog even more.

The trainer told them to keep calm, be assertive, and give the dog the feeling that they are in charge and safe. Stop talking to him, stop looking at him, stop giving him so much attention — and just walk!

Of course, it was like a miracle. As soon as they just took the dog for a walk without praising him all the time and making anxious noises, then he became quiet, confident and happy, and the problem began to disappear at a stroke. There was much work still to be done but the main thing was the demonstration of how energy and fear are picked up by others.

This is a bit of an extreme case but I use it not to compare dogs to children but to show the effect of nervous, anxious energy.

By being anxious themselves, this family had created two results; first, they gave the dog the impression that there is something to worry about and second, they were constantly giving the dog praise for being anxious, which enhanced that feeling of confusion in him ('You mean you like it when I am anxious?').

I have tried to stress how important it is to be calm, to feel calm, to emanate calmness. This is because children will pick up at once on your tension and it will make them anxious or excitable, or both. Not a good combination at all …

One of the problems with modern life for children is that there is always stimulation for them. Television programmes are always high energy and so are computer games; social media platforms play their part too. Sometimes it is wonderful for children to just lie down with a good book and look at the pictures or make up stories. They need time to be quiet but still creative and productive. More and more, I am seeing how the importance of being calm is hugely underestimated. However, I would add to this that nobody, man nor beast, can be calm if they are not getting enough freedom and exercise. You can be as relaxed as you like, but if your children are jumping out of their skins with frustration at not being able to play outside or at least to have physical play indoors, then it will all go to waste.

All living things respond well to calm and quiet environments. We have to find ways of not sharing our worries if they are based within ourselves. Somebody asked me at a seminar the other day: 'Surely we need to be open and honest with our children at all times?'. I agree with that, but not if it is our own difficulties or prejudices that are causing a problem. As we discussed earlier, this is the moment we need to evaluate ourselves and take steps to quell our own neurosis or fear, for it is only when we are sound and strong that we can truly help our children through anxious times or difficult moments.

I have two short stories here. One is when my daughter Amy was about two years old. We were out in a garden looking around and she came up to me with an ENORMOUS spider on her arm. Now I am not at all afraid of spiders, but the sight of that dear little girl with this huge creature on her soft little arm took me aback. I just had to control myself and stop myself from shouting: 'Aaaargh! You have a huge hairy spider on your arm!' Instead, I said quietly: 'Ooh, she's a lovely lady, isn't she. Shall we find somewhere nice to put her?'

We duly went off into the bushes and found a nice safe spot for Mrs Spider (she was undoubtedly a female because of her size) and let her go. My first reaction here was critical; it could have set the stage for her relationship with spiders for many years to come if I had reacted as my instinct first told me to respond.

The next story is about my son, Henry. He was and still is a great tree climber. One day I heard this little voice calling me: 'Mum, I'm up here'. It was Henry, aged ten, at the very top of the tallest tree in the area. I looked up and nearly fell over with panic to see him up there so high. Heights have never been good for me. I had to take control and look nonchalant because I obviously did not want to create tension in him while he negotiated the climb, so I looked up at him, waved and shouted a calm hello with a smile, and went back to sweeping my yard.

Talking to Henry today, he says that he had no idea at the time that I was so troubled by it … mission accomplished, Mum!

I am not suggesting that you let your children climb high trees; Henry happens to be extremely able — and safe — at climbing tall trees. This has to be an individual choice that is very dependent on their previous experiences, your level of anxiety and the layout of your area. However, I think it would be a shame not to let them ever climb trees at all.

Children do not need to be hyped up or made excited; they are perfectly capable of doing this for themselves. The most significant, single attribute contributing to a balanced, calm family is having quiet, calm adults. Perhaps unflappable is what I mean, not getting in a pickle every time something seems to be wrong and not responding to everything, either positive or negative. Grown-ups need to have their own lives, talk about adult things, read adult literature or listen to adult things on the radio. Of course, small children need some attention, but they do not need all the attention. Sometimes a little play in the garden or a short walk or look at a book and then they can be expected, quite reasonably, to amuse themselves for a while and not interrupt what the grown-ups are doing.

I think anxiety has a lot to do with the kind of tension I mean. The other day, I discussed this subject of remaining calm with Henry; I mimicked a parent getting anxious and telling a child to be careful of a hot fireplace. My voice rose, I spoke tensely, and my dog, who had been sleeping peacefully on the sofa, suddenly jumped up and stood looking anxious and confused. This was precisely the point I was making. Tension breeds tension. Because of my own nervous actions, I had created a tense situation that the dog picked up on and it frightened her. As with most animals, young children are very sensitive to energy, much more so than most adults are.

I think we all get angry with our children sometimes; it is natural and they are sure to get angry with us too, but it is important to let it go afterwards. No discussion, no talk, just forget it and move on. If they get angry with you, which is perfectly reasonable and fair, the same applies. Ignore it and move on, certainly don't raise it or dissect and discuss it afterwards.

We have an unwritten rule at Summerhill. 'What happens in the Meeting stays in the Meeting'. This means that you can bring things up against people and know that they won't be raised again after the Meeting. This is true of life as well. We all need the chance to express our irritation or rage without it being trawled out forever after for discussion and apologies.

Talking to children

The way that we talk to children, just as the way we talk to adults, sets the agenda of our relationship, the formation of trust, respect, truth and friendship.

Unfortunately for many people, there is an assumption that adults should talk differently to children, using a different tone, different attitude, and different content. An example of this is children's television programmes where 'jolly' adults talk, or often shout, to children in a patronising and cheerful way but with the brightness and body language that says the presenters are 'one of us' so we can all have lots of 'fun' together and be really whacky. Children do not need this kind of interaction with adults; they very often find it false and highly embarrassing.

Being equal to children is not helped by trying to be one of them. From my own experience, I would say that children both expect and like their adults to be adults. They are usually rather suspicious of anybody who ought to be behaving in a responsible adult way but is acting like a child instead. To be 'childlike and 'childish' are two completely different things; the former is to be able to identify and enjoy childish things, the latter is to be infantile and immature. Our children at Summerhill are very quick to pick out those, usually new, staff members who behave like this. They will generally hold little respect for such adults until they 'grow up'.

At Summerhill in 1999, we were busy preparing for a court clash against the UK government who were demanding changes to be made to the school's philosophy, which we were unwilling to make. We were creating policies to assist with our inspection process and to help explain how the school views the learning process at Summerhill. We took various papers to the children to ask for their feedback.

With the assessment policy, we felt that the children would very much want to be involved as it was about how we adults observed and monitored our pupils and therefore very personal to each of them as individuals. We called a Meeting to read through what we had written. A few of the older children turned up to our Meeting and we started going through the policy. After a few minutes, one of the oldest boys stood up and said that they were grateful for being asked about the procedure, but actually they trusted us adults to do the best thing for the school without it being intrusive to the pupils, and they would like to leave us to get on with it. The others agreed and they all, very politely, left the room.

I thought this was a perfect example of how free-range children think about adults, and I would undoubtedly have felt the same as a child. This is why, at Summerhill, we do not involve the children in the finances or business side of the school. We are not trying to create little adults, but we want our children to have a real childhood — a childhood with equality and freedom in order to flourish and gain confidence while not having to make decisions that they would find irrelevant to them as children.

Over years of experience, I have found that children have a genuine interest in what time they go to bed at night, but very little interest in who pays the electricity bills! This is the same in a family home setting.

I find that sometimes when I approach a new, perhaps rather timid child at Summerhill with my usual direct way of talking, they clam up for a moment, and I have to be quick to make a joke or two to make them realise that this grown-up is not what they thought she would be — 'The School Head'. I want to be able to talk to them in a relaxed and comfortable way, not worrying about 'getting it right' or if I am being too frank and open. I want to tease a bit in a very gentle way, have a bit of a laugh, and want to be absolutely straight with them. I hope that all the pupils at Summerhill and those from the past will know that whatever else — I am open and honest with them and that I will always shoot directly from the hip.

In my job this is useful on many levels. I may have to talk to a child about their parent's marriage break-up, illness in the family or perhaps a perceived eating problem. I will discuss this just as I would with one of the adults in the school — with sensitivity but absolute frankness.

The other day I was talking to a 16-year-old boy about his grandfather's terminal illness. We talked about how, of course, he would be allowed to visit home whenever he wanted, but also about how he might find it nice to get a bit of a break from the tension in the family while he was at school. He agreed with this, having found it quite a burden at home with the sadness of the rest of the family. He would still carry this sadness at school but would at least have other things to distract him.

I like to think that I am a bit of an expert on death, having lost all of my birth family as well as many, many good friends over the years, so we talked about how the death of his grandfather might be, about modern drugs and how these days we do not tend to get the old-fashioned death-bed scene with rattling breath and the family all around weeping. It was a very honest and straight conversation and I know that the boy really appreciated it. Of course, I would never have spoken to an 11-year-old in the same way.

Being equal does not mean allowing somebody to do as they wish in your home or your company. Sometimes we just have to tell somebody that what they are doing is out of line. It must be done with respect, just as you would talk to a colleague, with no ranting. I have said before, getting cross is all right provided that we act in an age-appropriate way and do not bully, threaten or intimidate anybody. I hope that your child would feel the same about you and be quite comfortable having a bit of an outburst from time to time. However, for me personally, I am happy to match a rise in energy if that is required. I do not take kindly to being shouted and screamed at, whether by an adult or a child, and I am quite comfortable with shouting back if I am verbally abused and it seems the right thing to do to create calm.

Sometimes things do have to be said. It is no good for either of you to bottle it up. Take, for instance, a teenager who may have left school and is going to college but still living at home. It could be that they spend a lot of time and money going out partying with friends or maybe even bringing them home. This situation might be all right for a while, but somebody will have to say something at some point. The freedom to be yourself can only go so far if it is infringing upon other people. I would feel that the most important thing would be not to make it an issue of 'what is best for you', or 'I think you ought to', but to attack the real problem, which is that I am fed up with having you around my house, not helping very much, not contributing to the family situation and then, on top of that, bringing home all your friends for noisy and expensive parties!

Time for a bit of straight-talking. Perhaps a cup of coffee and a kind but firm explanation of why this is not working for you, not for them, but for you. Remember, parents have rights too!

So often teenagers are not able to make real choices about what they do. Instead, they are 'expected' to take the route chosen by their parents. No wonder they sometimes get rebellious.

It is important to say what you want to children and not to nag or be boring. My father wanted me to stop smoking and I knew that. This was at the forefront of the time when cancer was being connected to smoking in a big way. He was afraid for me and wanted me to stop. Instead of railing at me, badgering me, he said, very frankly, that he wished I would stop because he could not bear to think that long after he was dead, I might die a horrible death of lung cancer. I did not stop immediately in response to this, but it certainly had a strong effect on how I viewed my smoking and will have influenced my eventual giving up for good at about twenty-six. I also knew that my father would have liked me to go to university and get a degree. He never told me that, but I just knew it. I am sure that it mattered an awful lot to him as he was an intellectual man and he wanted me to come back and run Summerhill one day. He mentioned that the school authorities would demand the person in charge to have qualifications, but I had no wish to go along that academic route.

My life was far more practical than that — I wanted to work with horses. I took my British Horse Society teaching exam and then another more advanced exam and became a riding instructor. During all the time I was doing this, my father only showed great pride and interest in what I was doing, though animals and their psychology were a complete mystery to him.

Why mention this? Because too many, far too many, parents think that they ought to have some sort of control over their children's futures. Somehow, we very often believe that we know best just because we are grown up. Of course, that gives us a level of life experience, but teenagers have the enthusiasm, idealism and courage of the young to bring to the table as well. Going back to us being the shepherds — we should be supporting them, advising them, helping them — and, yes, being realistic as well. When your daughter says that she intends to be a brain surgeon after spending all her time in her room playing heavy metal, then maybe, just maybe, it is time to get real and have that face-to-face honest talk about what she really wants to do with her life!

We should never be afraid to be open and honest with children. I think at Summerhill, this is one of our great strengths. Calling a spade, a spade, being straight, and feeling able to get cross, so long as the children have the same freedom to be cross with us.

It is not as though we are all going around shouting at one another or getting angry willy-nilly. But it is a place where you can express annoyance in a way that adults cannot do in most teaching environments. The sort of thing I am talking about is perhaps a staff member who has been kept awake at night for a while and is coming to the end of their tether, feeling that the community is not taking the problem seriously. They need to know that it is all right to show genuine emotion about it, to cry if they want to, to show how they feel about the situation. Children can deal with it and they also need to know that we are human with all the usual human failings and faults.

I remember one of the house-parents on the top corridor (ages 10-13) calling a Special Meeting one morning. He was tired out and started to cry. He told the children that what was a bit of fun to them, playing up after bedtime and making noise, was really hurting him. He said he had to get up the next day, he had to do a job of work and he had reached the end of his tether. This was a Meeting when there were no arguments or excuses. Everybody was very subdued. This man was much loved and respected by all in the school. They could see, these noisy House kids, that they had pushed him too far and they clearly felt bad about it.

Obviously, we must all show some restraint. An angry adult can be intimidating and frightening for a child or teenager and nobody should ever step across that line. If they did that in Summerhill, they might well be brought up in the school Meeting, as happened recently when a teacher was felt to have been overly aggressive in his manner when talking to one of the pupils. He was given a medium work fine (40 minutes supervised work around the grounds) and a Strong Warning to be careful and not do it again.

We must never go down the road of making huge mountains out of molehills. Children come up with many ideas, fads and misunderstandings in their young lives. It is best to keep a very level head and a calm attitude to all of these. If a child were to decide, for example, to become a vegan (or if the family were vegans and they chose to eat meat), we should just try to take it as it comes, no fuss, no big discussions, no flapping about. Just go quietly with the flow. The child will either enjoy the experience and remain eating that way or pass through it and go back to their own default setting. Either way, it is not really our business if you think about it.

If it is something bigger than eating, maybe something life-changing, then we have to be extra careful not to make a huge deal about it and rush off for counselling. It should take a long time for a young person to know exactly where they want to be with big decisions. We should try to give them time and space and good old 'down-to-earth' practical discussion so that there is time to let things develop naturally.

But also keep in mind, in a good-humoured sort of way, that teenagers by their very nature are great dramatists! They love to create and take part in performances, and sometimes the very idea of having to seek professional help can be a bit of an exciting thing. So, I don't say that you should not seek help, but perhaps just make sure that it is left for a while to see if it wears off and in case it is just one of those little dramas. That is not belittling a young person's anxieties at all; it is merely being realistic and giving them time to come to that conclusion if that is where it was going to go anyway. Surprising how often a young person will say to you a year later that they are embarrassed about a particular time or action in their life. Then it can be good to have a bit of warm, loving laughter about it and perhaps tell them about some of your own misdemeanours in your murky past!

We have had a number of pupils who have proposed in the school Meeting that their name was changed. The proposal is always carried. Sometimes it lasts for their whole time at school and into their future lives, but sometimes it only lasts a matter of days. I remember being called Daisy for a while because I did not like the name Zoë. I was probably about eight at the time. I cannot remember how long it lasted, probably about three days, but it was my own ability to be who I wanted to be that was important and to have it ratified by the school Meeting.

There have also been a few pupils who have talked about gender change during their time with us. Everybody just treats it normally and makes no fuss, giving them time to come to their own decision about who they feel they want to be. I have not seen anybody take that step yet as they usually move on to being happy within their own gender but can fashion it to control this in the way they want that gender to be perceived. Again, it is not important to anybody but themselves, and although as youngsters they might need to be steadied and slowed down, in the end (and I would hope this is not to be until they were in their twenties), it must be their own decision.

There seems to be a big swing at the moment towards talking to children about being 'depressed'. Again, this is something that I have serious issues with. I am certainly not implying that young people do not get depression, but I think that we need to put it in perspective. As I keep on saying, we need to normalise it first to see if it can be worked through as a natural emotion before we go down the route of seeking external professional help.

Modern thinking seems very often to confuse sadness with depression. There is going to be a lot of sadness in most of our lives and I think that not recognising it for what it is will do us no good at all. Sadness is a good, though difficult, thing to deal with; it is normal and natural to grieve, about minor things, about large things. We must also remember that being a teenager is a very explosive time and our emotions can run riot. Calm and grounded can very often, in my experience, be the answer to helping teenagers through these difficult times. It all goes back to leadership. Keeping a calm air of authority, not over the child but over the situation you all find yourself in, will help build a good, composed outcome.

Properly diagnosed clinical depression is another ball game altogether and needs help and support. Figuring out which of these is raising its ugly head can be a difficult one for parents and families in the early stages. I feel that the advice above is the best way forward at the start with children and young people; keep calm, don't jump to conclusions, and be careful not to create a label because it will be very hard to 'un-label' again. Let us just assume it is sadness to begin with and then go on, very slowly, from there, rather than flying off to the professionals at the first hint of a problem.

Some local authorities are very good at keeping a lid on things and will not allow young people to go onto drugs or therapy until they have gone through a time of following a solid timetable and self-help regime. Still, I have seen the occasional parents who have gone through the private medicine route and obtained drugs very early on in the programme, which I think is outrageous.

Justice and fairness

Summerhill has been described as the oldest children's democracy in the world. Justice is something that is really important to us at Summerhill. We do not want to punish our community members as such, but it is important that we mark the moment with a sanction of some sort, not only for the future of their behaviour but also to give the victim a feeling of justice having been done, drawing a line in the sand if you like.

Children take fairness and justice very seriously; it is important to them, probably much more than we adults remember. Of all the things that concern children, I think their sense of fairness and justice — different though these two concepts are — runs at a very high level. The fact that Summerhill children can take things to the Meeting and bring things up gives them a sense of justice. It is not about punishing the person who rode your bicycle; it is about you getting a fair hearing, about making it clear to the other person that it was not okay for them to steal your bike, and you do not want them to do it again. In other words, justice denotes conduct that is morally required.

It is also about your feeling that you have said what you wanted to say, you have been listened to, and people have taken note of it. The perpetrator also needs to shed any guilt about what they did and feel that life can go back to normal; fairness denotes an evaluative judgment as to whether the justice meted out was morally praiseworthy. All the time, we are learning that hard fact of life — that none of us can do just what we want to all the time. Freedom as opposed to licence!

Justice and fairness in the home are also essential because one child will often feel that another child in the family is getting a different deal, a better deal than they are. We have to be careful to be fair and reasonable with everybody and not be picking on one person because they are younger or older or male or female.

Once again, we all think that we are doing this well and are being fair, but there is always time to stop and look, evaluate and think — am I really treating everybody equally?

I think of a young woman I spoke to recently in her mid-teens who comes from a liberal and very, very loving family. In the course of our conversation, she said that she has always been the one who was told off. Her younger sister always got away with everything and had everything she wanted. She feels that whenever there was a problem, it was always her fault. Now she feels a real sense of injustice. I don't know whether this is just perceived, and her parents may well say that it was not like this, but my point is that if she feels that it is happening, then it is happening. So once again, we poor parents need to look at ourselves and ask if we are doing this as well as we can! What could we be doing that might be creating a sense of injustice here for our children, a feeling of imbalance, and are we being fair and reasonable to everybody?

I listened to an old tape recording I had of my children when they were tiny. The youngest one was talking baby talk and giving a message to his daddy. The older two were chipping in and saying bits and bobs as well. As I listened, I was appalled to hear that I was talking baby talk to the younger one and encouraging him to chatter while at the same time I seemed to be rather dismissive of the older two. Could that really be me? I was thoroughly ashamed of myself.

You have obviously got to be a little bit age aware. A two-year-old needs to be looked after more than a five-year-old, and a two-year-old needs some understanding that a five-year-old does not need. You have to be creative and find ways to make sure that both parties feel equal and not picked on, and not forget that two-year-olds can be quite wily at times and not always the little innocents that we tend to think they are!

With my own children, I always tried to make the actual dispute the villain and not pick sides. It was the argument itself that was the problem, not the individuals. I would have an expectation that they could and should be trying to sort out issues rather than just shrieking at one another.

When they were little (probably under four), I had a cupboard in the kitchen, which held a lot of toys and things to do. These were mummy's things. So, they could use them and play with them, but there was no room for argument because they were not actually the owners and thus had to try and find ways to negotiate and compromise. It was really useful and they were very happy with the way it worked. It also helped a bit with keeping things relatively tidy (I was never house-proud). 'Please put my things away' is much easier than 'Put YOUR things away' and makes great sense to the children. If a serious row occurred, I would just quietly put my things away in the cupboard until everybody was happy to start over again.

Swearing

Let's talk about something that most people prefer not to talk about in families. This is going to be a bit of a controversial one inside families. I want to talk about bad language or profanities I believe they are called in some circles. Most people know it as swearing, and although many do it from time to time, one thing is for sure, children must NEVER, EVER swear!

But actually, I have some news — children do it as well. They swear all the time. Among themselves, on the internet, behind the bike sheds at school and when they are out together, socialising.

It seems to be one of the great myths, or should I say, another of the great childhood myths that adults continue to perpetuate. I am never sure if it is just denial, naivety or down-right wishful thinking. It is something that needs to be addressed and faced up to. If we are to have a good working relationship with our children, then we certainly need to be able to talk about the issue of swearing, and we need to be able to discuss it entirely openly. Just putting a blanket ban on it is a complete waste of time because you have absolutely no way of upholding that ban. I am a firm believer that if you want to make rules, it is no good making them and then not being able to maintain them — what a waste of energy and time, and what a terrible lesson for life.

So, let us look at a scenario that is probably quite unlikely to happen in most homes, but it could.

One day your 14-year-old daughter tells you that you are a fucking bitch. How do you deal with it?

Swearing is such a big issue for many adults. Although they probably swear themselves, they have a problem with children swearing. It is all tied up with the idea of children needing protection from the realities of life, which we talked about earlier, and also of being 'robbed' of their childhood. The expression 'robbed of their childhood' is one often bandied around when people think that children are having their innocence 'taken away'. I have never been entirely clear about what this innocence is supposed to be and how on earth you can take innocence away.

If anything is robbing children of their childhood, I would have thought it was the universally accepted education systems with their constant demands of academic attainment and lack of natural, free, creative play, but that is another subject ...

At Summerhill, everybody is allowed to swear if they wish. However, there is a firm understanding that you cannot swear AT somebody or offend anybody by your language. So, whereas in the world at large, swearing often tends to be rather aggressive and usually aimed directly at a person, at Summerhill, it is very much a 'throw-away' kind of statement. For instance, the sort of thing you might do if you hit your finger with a hammer. If you were to swear AT somebody, then you would certainly be brought up in the school Meeting.

Basically, a child swearing is not something that we adults have control over. Your kids will swear among their friends whether you like it or not. You can either take the usual route, which is to forbid it or take a more sensible way, which is to bring it out in the open so that it can be discussed.

So, back to your daughter telling you that you are a fucking bitch: the Summerhill angle is that you obviously have no authority to tell her what language she may or may not use. That is her own freedom of choice, but of course you have the right not to hear it if you wish, and as she was using it in an aggressive way towards you, that was not alright either. There clearly needs to be some discussion about this situation.

How about telling her that it is not okay to do it in front of you? You could also point out that it might be better if she didn't use this kind of language in front of the neighbours, Mr Brown down the road or Great Aunt Hermione, as any of those people might be very offended by it. Along with this, you have to make it clear that this is something that she needs to take control over and act responsibly using it. It is her life and her decision to use whatever language she likes, but she needs to know that as a person, she ought to have good manners (basic, good manners, not the kind of thing that people usually call good manners such as letting the ladies go first or pulling out chairs for people to sit down). Having good manners means thinking about how other people will feel about what we say and do and trying not to offend them by our actions if at all possible. You may feel comfortable saying that you do not want her to use foul language when she is within your earshot or in the family house.

I know many Summerhill children who never swear in the holidays or when they go to their grandparent's house. Our children at school are not allowed to swear in the local town or when there are tradespeople working at school. It is not rocket science to be able to control your language in different situations; mostly, if allowed to, children tend to swear somewhat less than we think they would. I would add to this that if it has been off-limits and you decide to take the big

Your kids will swear among their friends, whether you like it or not ...
the best response is to open it up for discussion.

step to open it to a family discussion, then you should be prepared for a few days of your child trying to shock you — it just goes with the territory and the best thing to do is to totally ignore it unless it is offending a relative or family friend.

Sometimes a new parent of Summerhill will contact me to ask what they should do as their young child is coming home from Summerhill and using a lot of bad language. It is usually because another new pupil has wound them up and taught them a lot of words just to cause shock. I always tell them to play it down and follow the above format and it will soon stop, which it always does.

My granddaughter, aged five, was very quick to make sure that her little sister did not swear at her nursery school and was careful to tell us all where we could and could not use bad language. Woe betide anybody who did not take heed of her!

My father told a lovely story about me when I was a little lass of about four. I had been told that I could not swear in front of visitors. One day there was an old friend of the family visiting and I was trying to do something that was not working — I said loudly 'F …', and then stopped abruptly, looked up at her and asked: 'Are you a visitor?' She said that she was a friend. I said, 'Oh Fuck!'

Before you throw your hands up in horror, let's look at what all this actually means. First, if you open it up for discussion, then it means that you are not making useless rules that will surely be broken anyway. 'You aren't allowed to swear' is something that you can't possibly achieve, so what is the point of going along that route?

Explaining your reasons for not wanting to hear people swearing is fine — but you have to make sure this really is a two-way discussion and that you are not talking 'at' your daughter. She has to understand what you mean precisely, and you can ask that she respects this. In a sensible situation where the family has a good working relationship regarding equality of status, your daughter will be only too happy to comply with your proposal. But she may have requests of her own — such as: 'Mum, when we are out in public, will you please stop correcting the way I talk/telling me not to forget to put my coat on/treating me like I am a baby — because it really embarrasses me'.

Okay, so fair's fair, now you have to be prepared to make those changes too. That is part of the deal.

Family clashes

My daughter Amy told me about when her own children were young and had a small 'problem' with supper. She had cooked the food as usual; the kids were watching TV, came in, looked at the food, didn't want any and went back to the TV again. They were aged five and three. Amy lost her cool and was cross. 'What is the point of cooking food for you to eat if you are too busy watching TV to bother to eat it. You will be hungry later'. Of course, she was right about this.

No problem with being cross about a situation provided that you are not tyrannising or frightening. It is important to show your feelings — so long as you are prepared to listen to and accept your children's anger when they feel it towards you.

Later they talked about it in a reasonable, quiet way. Amy explained that she was fed up with making food for them when they weren't going even to try to eat it. Her perception of the situation was that the kids were just too distracted to take supper seriously. The outcome of this was that they all decided the TV should be switched off at suppertime and this seemed to work out well.

Some families battle with the problem of messiness. Mess is a problem that faces all parents and is a difficult one to resolve. At Summerhill, we have cleaning staff who come in each day and clean all the main areas of the school. The reasons for this are twofold: it is a matter of health and safety, and we have to keep the school clean just because it is a school.

We know from experience that kids don't happily keep their areas tidy, so rather than create a problem that would be ongoing and probably irresolvable, we choose to keep the school tidy another way. However, although the cleaners give a sweep around and a tidy-up in the younger children's rooms, the older one's rooms are their own responsibility. There are special 'Room Ombudsmen' who keep an eye on general tidiness which is beyond the cleaner's remit, and we also have a committee called 'Health and Safety' who go around a few times each term to check that rooms are not a health hazard, that light fittings, etc. are safe. This committee of seven can comprise kids and adults. It always has somebody experienced with things like fire hazards on the committee.

As for the outside of the school, we have regular work fines, which are very useful for picking up litter and we will occasionally resort to an all-school clean-up which involves all of us clearing up for about half an hour. It is not compulsory.

At home, I always tried to keep things on a personal basis between my children and myself, rather than making it a moral one. So, cleaning up was not something which 'ought' to be done, but rather something I wanted help with because otherwise, I would have to do it all myself. The reality is that if you have little children, you have to be prepared to do the cleaning and tidying. Make the space as easy as possible; preferably give them a room to themselves where they can make a mess that you might only attack once a week or so.

You have to be realistic and remember that in a balanced home, the parents and kids both have rights, whilst also understanding the nature of childhood and that children really don't notice mess, so it is not important to them. Try to get a balance. I don't mind the grandchildren having a good game and piling the cushions up on the settee or spreading toys around, I am very happy to clear up after them, but if they get rowdy in my house, I tell them not to. After all, it is my house!

Sometimes, parents imagine that children need to learn about cleaning up to make them tidy adults in the future. We do not expect our children to cook our food to become good cooks, so learning to tidy up is a bit of a weak point. Living in a tidy house that is kept clean by the adults is more likely to breed a person who likes living tidily, if you think about it.

At Summerhill, we have ombudsmen and the school Meetings to deal with conflict, but it is not that simple in private homes. Trying to be an impartial observer is difficult but must be the priority. It helps if you can take a stance about your own personal space, such as: 'Come on you lot, stop all this arguing; it drives me nuts when you keep bickering.' With younger children, it should be the argument itself that is the crime — that way, you don't take sides.

Try to sort out a compromise whenever possible, keep a good sense of humour about it, make light and amusing of the situation without mocking anybody. Most important is to remember that bickering is the nature of the beast with little children — that's how they learn about conflict and compromise, so it is always a good learning experience!

They will argue and pick on one another, there will be tears; that's the way it goes. Try not to let it get you down, keep your sense of humour.

Don't always presume that the older one is the problem; younger kids wind older ones up both accidentally and on purpose. Try to be fair at all times.

These are all things that Summerhill Ombudsmen will be doing every day as they sort out a myriad of problems between both big and small children. Some seem to be very petty to us as adults, but they all have to be taken seriously, though children do have to learn that some things are really petty and should be swallowed down and forgotten. The old saying that sticks and stones may break my bones but names will never hurt me is actually a pretty good one.

Bedtime is a difficult area for most families. At Summerhill, we have bedtimes set by the school Meeting and bedtimes officers to enforce them, with fines for those that break the laws. Our bedtimes are set pretty late compared to most families:

The youngest (age 6-9) go to bed at 8 pm with lights out at 8:30 pm and a half-hour later in the summer term and at weekends (Friday and Saturday).

The next ones (age 9-11) have bedtime at 9.00 pm lights out 9.30 pm. Half an hour later at weekends.

The next group (about 11-13) has bedtime at 10 pm and lights out at 10.30 pm with weekends at 10.30 pm to 11 pm.

The next group (aged 13-15) — has bedtime at 10.30 pm and can keep their lamps on until 11 pm. Friday 11 pm-11.30 pm. Saturday 11.30-midnight.

The oldest children (up to 17 or 18) have a bedtime at 11:30 pm when they have to be in their rooms but can keep the light on. They have no bedtime on nights before slobbing days (days when you do not have to get up in the mornings) but have to be in their area after 11:30 pm.

At Summerhill, we also have 'wake up' at 8.00 am when the bedtimes officers wake everybody (including the staff), and if you are still not up at 8:30 am, you get a fine. This can be, for example, going to the back of the lunch queue, a small money fine or having a screen ban for 24 hours.

Sometimes these laws will change, Shack kids (age 13-15) sometimes get to be allowed to walk around their rooms after bedtime or keep their lamps on for longer, or watch TV — but all of those considerations would be dependent upon them being respectful of the laws in the first place. The bedtime rules generally don't change very much. Although the younger ones regularly bring up that they would like a later bedtime, the rest of the community feels that they need sleep, and the motion is dropped.

It is different in a private home where you have no bedtimes officers to put people to bed because it brings us back to the old adult/child conflict situation. It can be hard when children have to get up early to go to school and are tired from the night before, and most parents understandably feel the need to put their foot down. I think with older children it is always worth talking the problem through and explaining your own difficulties, perhaps like getting them up in the morning for school and so on. Again, maybe a compromise at the weekend is a good idea.

Power struggles

One of the problems repeatedly raising its head in modern child-rearing is the continual push-me-pull-you over power and control between adults and children. In most modern child-rearing systems, parents are expected to protect and control their children, while children must learn from and obey their parents. That sounds pretty simple, but in reality, the road is often clouded with difficulties.

In some families, the situation runs smoothly because whatever problems arise are ironed out relatively easily. But in many other families there is heartache, anger and misunderstanding, causing much worry and insecurity for adults and children alike. Interestingly, many parents feel instinctively uncomfortable about their all-powerful role. Many very traditional parents voice concerns about the direction they give and their children's lack of power over their own destinies. This can lead to a very modern problem: giving too much decision-making to the children without any real thought about boundaries.

We can often end up with the proverbial 'spoilt brat' situation where the child calls all the shots and behaves tyrannically. Parents can be afraid to be more assertive. This is very often because they do not, under any circumstances, want to be the kind of parents of previous generations; in shying away from that, but without enough preparation and information, mistakes can be made. Parents often need help and guidance to deal with this situation, and they need to feel comfortable reassessing their approach and not take it personally when things seem to break down.

In past times children have taken very different roles in society. Elizabethan children, for instance, were treated very much the same as adults. They were not protected from sights and experiences in the same way as today's children, being able to talk about adult subjects, play adults sports and games, and even attend executions.

People say that children grow up so fast these days. Actually, in medieval times boys were expected to work and could be hanged for theft at seven. You could marry at fourteen and serve in the army at 15. Citizens as young as 12 could serve on juries. At the battle of Crecy (1346), the command of the vanguard — the first battalion of the army — was given to Prince Edward at 16 years of age.[2]

---

2 *Ian Mortimer, The Time Traveller's Guide to Medieval England*

In the early days of Summerhill, between the two world wars, my father had very different children to deal with compared to today. There was an acceptance that children should be reared with firm discipline, often being told to 'wait until your father comes home' so that they could receive a dressing down or a thrashing; Neill banned all corporal punishment from day one of Summerhill in 1921.

In those early days of the school, there was much less emotion shown even to other family members than we see today. Society was so strong and the class structure more rigid that very few people rebelled against the expectations demanded of them. Children were expected to be seen and not heard, and they, as well as adults in the community, were kept in their places for fear of what other people might think. Of course, this led to much unhappiness that continued into adult life — many repressions were unable to be lifted, and a cycle of controlled behaviour and internal frustration and anger became the norm for many people.

Today's families have a different problem. They have lost their way somewhat in the childrearing maze. Even though the 'old days' were authoritarian and repressive, there was at least a security in knowing where everybody stood in the hierarchy of life and social order. Of course, many of the systems were absolutely unacceptable: the baby-rearing in the early part of this century when mothers might sit on the stairs weeping but afraid to go and feed their desperately crying baby because the 'four hours between feeds' advocated by Truby King was in force. The children were learning in school by rote and getting beaten across the knuckles (or worse) for not knowing their times tables.

All of this, we now agree, was oppressive, and corporal punishment was barbaric. But what have we done to replace these methods? There have, over the years, been some excellent, authoritative books such as Dr Spock's child-rearing manual[3]. These helped to turn the tide and create more humane methods. But most have wafted away in the mists of time. I don't suppose that any modern parents have even heard of Dr Spock!

---

3 *Baby & Child Care, Dr Spock 1946, told parents to love and respond to their babies, to feed them when they wanted to feed and to trust their own instincts more. This was in direct opposition to the earlier manuals of the likes of Truby King.*

*If we ordered adults to eat something they loathed,
it would be seen as unreasonable bullying.*

These days many families might approach things more randomly. It is not unusual to see a child called from their sumptuous bedroom, complete with TV, video, stereo, internet connection, computer or games console, to a family meal where they are told that they must eat all their greens. This child will argue in a sullen or aggressive way and may easily get away without eating their greens. But the conflict is still there. The parents are still trying to maintain authority over something which should actually be the child's own choice, and the child is acting defiantly and disagreeably to that authority. So a kind of acceptance of bullying from both sides and unpleasantness in the home becomes normal.

At Summerhill, we never have to face these trivial battles, only because we know that they are unreasonable. What right do I, as an adult, have to tell a child what they have to eat? It is illogical that anybody could tell someone else what to eat unless it is on genuine medical grounds.

How would you, the reader, feel if I invited you to dinner, made a dish which you loathe and then demanded, no, ordered you to eat it all up? Why is it acceptable because the other person is a child, somebody physically smaller and mentally less mature than yourself? If this did happen in an adult context, it would be seen as unreasonable bullying.

But, a problem just as common is that of providing anything on the menu that a child might want. 'I don't like that' is a common thing to hear from children. The correct answer? 'Well then, go without. There is plenty of bread and cheese in the kitchen if you are hungry.'

It is sometimes a shock to adults who have expectations of what children should be eating to grow strong and healthy to hear that many smaller children at Summerhill might, for instance, eat mainly carbohydrates for a lot of the time and take no harm at all to their health. The food issue can create massive conflict and is often because a child quickly realises that they can have power over their own lives because nobody can physically force them to eat! If parents calmed down about it right at the start, then things would go a whole lot better. It is equally bad to provide anything that the child wants because of anxiety about their health.

There are many times when we have children arrive at Summerhill and are told that they are lactose intolerant or unable to eat this or that. Very often within a few weeks, this child has forgotten about it, cannot be bothered to go for their 'special' milk and just gulps down what is on the table at break time, remaining as fit as a fiddle.

At Summerhill, we have seen a great number of faddy eaters go through many phases of eating and come out at the other end as strong, healthy young adults with a well-balanced attitude to food and a discerning palate.

So, power struggles, though they need careful handling at the start if you are re-learning your parental role, need never actually be power struggles at all — just communication, negotiation and compromise, hopefully with a good measure of warmth, love and humour thrown in as well.

Boundaries

Safety in our home was always paramount, but my children grew up in a farmyard with a large, unfenced pond in the middle. Nobody fell in it. When a friend's son, aged about 10, came to play with them one day, it was not long before he slipped off the edge into the water while playing the fool. It was as though he was so unaccustomed to taking risks that his judgment was not as acute as it should have been. Watching him at play he seemed clumsily quite unaware of his own physical capabilities. My children were gobsmacked!

When they were toddlers, we had a safe area, but they were responsible enough to be sensible as they grew older, even though they did push the boundaries somewhat; a wooden pallet raft springs to mind. I think it was older brother Will's invention and he boldly paddled himself and younger Henry out across the water. They had such fun with it, floating around the pond, wobbling dangerously with a wonky pole as an oar. I found an old photograph of it the other day and shuddered at my youthful confidence in them!

But I was right and I would do it again. You cannot wrap your children up safely, and doing so will be seriously detrimental to their future lives. There is still a frayed rope hanging from a tree where they used to swing out over the water. Terrifying stuff for parents, but you sometimes have to try and curb your anxieties and your parental programming of 'what if' and let the children take some risks. The horrible truth is that even if you wrap them in cotton wool, it will do them no good. You have to experience being in some danger in life in order to learn how to stop when your own safety valves tell you to stop.

We would never have let our children take silly risks, but I cannot recall feeling that I needed to intervene, other than perhaps to remind them that straw stacks can be unstable and to keep an eye open for wobbly bales. There will be tumbles, a few bruises — but I have seen at Summerhill that if a nasty fall occurs (and it is very rare indeed), it is borne with some pride and considered a worthwhile battle scar by those who have them! I remember feeling a bit ashamed when we were children comparing battle scars as I had none — until I attempted to stop a couple of tomcats from fighting and got a very nasty bite for my trouble, which left me a fine scar I bear to this day.

Don't keep telling your child what not to do. If you don't want them to do stuff, then put it out of the way. If it is not dangerous, irritating or unpleasant to other people, then let them do it!

I am wary of saying this as one of the things that infuriates me is seeing children throwing their weight around, being loud and pushy. Time and time again, I have watched children being disrespectful and ignoring constant requests to cease certain behaviours by parents who seem incapable of just saying it like it is — 'Stop being an idiot, you simply cannot behave like this.'

In a pupil's early days at Summerhill, any social difficulties he or she displays are almost all because the child has not had firm, clear boundaries in their lives. They do not understand the concept of living respectfully with other people. Of course, a certain amount of this is normal and about learning one's own boundaries and those of other people, an ongoing process in growing up (especially if they are the only child in the family). But some of it is also due to being indulged, and this is the hardest for the school community to deal with.

Give the children some space

Allow children to be quiet, calm, inquiring. Let them get on with their own lives. Actually, very small children like and need to have space alone without stimulation from adults.

As I mentioned earlier, I have a huge problem with children's television shows because the presenters constantly talk in a jerky, hyped-up fashion. It first shows a complete lack of knowledge about children and their needs and brings tension and excitement into every home, just when children often need to wind down after school or other daytime excitement. I think the perfect presenter was surely the fictional Mrs Doubtfire from the film of the same name, starring Robin Williams. She spoke to children like people — intelligent people, just small, inexperienced ones, that's all.

So, I always advise parents to not respond to every murmur their child makes or keep up a running chit-chat throughout their playing, and certainly don't react to everything they do, in either a positive or a negative way.

We all need to become accustomed to gaining our own pleasure from doing things without expecting constant feedback. Children need to be able to enjoy their own process without input from an adult. One of my particular bugbears is the idea that we need to shower praise upon our children for every little thing they do — to 'give them confidence'. There is no greater confidence than that gained for ourselves, by ourselves. Sure, it is nice to have successes shared and confirmed, but our first joy must be in our own ability.

After the toddler age, children need their own time and space to experience successes and failures in their games or building projects without the constant support and praise from an adult. Obviously, if your child is on their own, then you will need to have some interaction; otherwise they might feel lonely, and nobody is saying that children should spend all their time on their own, just that they should be able to have that time and even be encouraged to. Praising children is fine too — but maybe save it for the grand finale?

Something frequently said at Summerhill by pupils is that they feel free to be quiet, bored, and alone. For many of them, this has been the first time in their lives because their school or home life has never catered for this need. It is not unusual to see a child sitting on the swing all alone, just sitting there.

Visitors have asked me: 'That child looks sad, why is nobody going to check on her?'

Why? Because she wants to be alone. Children are perfectly able to decide if they want company or not. If she needs help, she will come to somebody and get it.

Last year we had a five-year-old who spent many hours cycling around by herself, exploring, watching, happy. She was not a loner and often played with friends, but she just loved being by herself. Until coming to Summerhill from other schools, most children will have been directed rather a lot, and they can feel a bit lost when suddenly they find themselves having to make their own entertainment. They soon become accustomed to it and feel able to find their own interests. I remember having periods of boredom when I was a child at Summerhill when I was just not motivated enough to find anything particular to do; however, if anybody had suggested something for me, I would probably have turned it down!

One of our staff, Michael, told me a story about how he had been watching from his window one day and a very small girl, our only five-year-old at the time, had been playing all by herself out on the field. She looked so happy, so calm and so self-contained that he just watched her in wonder. Afterwards, he said that he felt a bit intrusive to have been observing her and had turned away so that she would be truly alone.

When things go a bit wrong at home, we adults tend to get annoyed and start analysing, explaining and reasoning with our children. But actually, children aren't much interested in talking about feelings and behaviour or why they did something they should not have done. What they care about is relevant stuff — 'I'm bored, I'm too cold, I'm hungry'. They don't want analysis, or reasoning, or 'sitting down together and talking everything over', in a grown-up fashion.

A quick explanation to clarify things is good:

'Daddy is jumping up and down, waving his arms and screaming because you have just dropped his laptop into the compost bin'.

I think it's fine, in fact it is good to be cross if you feel cross, who wouldn't be? But let it be simple. Let it be about my laptop and the compost bin, not about 'why did you do that' or 'let's talk about being thoughtless and unkind'.

Neill told a story about one of his pupils digging up his potatoes without asking. Neill went to the school Meeting and was very angry. People might criticise this — being angry with a child, but he was making the same point. He was angry, not about a naughty child but about his potatoes, nothing else. No morality or guilt trips, they were his potatoes. I cannot drop your laptop onto the compost bin, and equally, you cannot dig up someone else's potatoes!

Summerhill Meetings tend to reflect this attitude. Mostly they are non-judgmental and straightforward. 'You shouldn't have done that; you get a 20-minute litter-pick-up as a fine', end of the issue. Bish-Bash-Bosh!

We sometimes get a pupil at Summerhill who says, 'I cannot help getting angry and when I get angry I cannot control myself'. I am guessing they have been led to believe this by well-meaning adults, parents or teachers. Sometimes they will use the excuse of having ADHD or some similar condition.

I hear a number of parents talk about how their children cannot control their anger for one reason or another. They will often discuss this with the child and offer help and advice about how to calm themselves down or about how to 'manage' their anger. The problem with this is that it accentuates the problem, or rather, it makes it into a problem. Yes, we can all control our anger. It is not always easy, but even a child can do it given time.

At Summerhill, there is never any question about it. Sometimes a person will be brought up in the school Meeting for some kind of temper led behaviour and may offer the excuse that they are a person who cannot control their anger. The response of the Meeting will always be:

'Well, yes actually, you can control your anger; everybody can control it. So stop making excuses and jolly well just get on and do it!'

And after a time, it always works. It may sound like a hard lesson, but this is a reality in life. We may do different things and have different thoughts and ideas; we may take different paths and have different personalities, but we are all human and we share the same traits, instincts, emotions and intuitions that our ancestors have shared for millions of years. So our first skill must be communication and compromise with other people.

Most of us do not think about the time that it takes to actually grow up. We tend to think of childhood as being over once children reach their late teens. I would dispute this after watching so many children grow and mature at Summerhill and beyond.

Young people continue to grow and mature for many years. Very often, the things that we worry about with our children — their plans, motivation, courage, assertiveness, to name just a few, will come along a lot more slowly than we thought they would.

I think of my daughter, Amy, a true Summerhill girl born and bred who was always what most people would have termed a quiet sort of girl. She was no wallflower, did several acting roles and flourished within her group but would not readily have pushed herself forward. As she grew up, she got stronger and stronger. According to some of her peers at the time, she became quite a scary 'big kid', particularly amongst a certain group of boys who liked to challenge the school bedtime rules!

It makes me laugh now to watch her at work on the farm when quaking seed representatives or corn buyers have to face Amy and negotiate her best prices. Whilst totally charming in her manner, she is a force to be reckoned with in all departments and is sure to screw them down to the very tightest deal possible!

Having that background of being able to define ourselves and to know that we are important is a powerful thing, whether we learned it in our family homes or our schools or both. Sometimes it can take a bit of time to emerge, but with a strong background of equality and the confidence gained from that, it will come out in the end if it is allowed to.

Accepting children for who they really are

Every parent wants to believe that their own child is special — honest, honourable and kind. But there might be times in a child's life when they are not actually very nice. We notice at Summerhill that children will sometimes try on a few different personalities and wear them for a while over some time while they discover whether they like them or not.

As mentioned earlier, we quite often see children change their names (a very common one), become thieves and take small things off their roommates or friends; they may become bullies in a minor sense or general law-breakers. Occasionally they might hang out with a group of people that would normally seem incompatible with their personalities. It is all about growing up, about trying things on for size and, more often than not, finding that the old outfit was probably the one that you liked the best. Sometimes they go from the bad to the good, so to speak. A grumpy, angry young person can suddenly find themselves with a group of positive new friends and make a complete transformation.

For parents or any adults for that matter, this can be a bit of a painful thing to watch. We all did it. We all went through those phases and I am sure that we all find it toe-curling to look back on it. Those: 'Oh, no, I didn't do that, did I?' moments are probably best forgotten!

As always, having a good sense of fun and keeping it light is the very best way to deal with it. I am not saying you don't take a young person seriously, but I am saying that these are phases, and if you do not react too strongly but keep a cool head, it will all sort out in the end.

Being a parent or working with children, we need to be ready to accept them for what they really are and give them our support and unconditional love no matter what they do. This does not mean allowing them to do whatever they like or approving of everything they do. It is fine to tell a child if you think they have been wrong, but so important that they know you still love them. Strong boundaries are crucial, but emotional judgment must be taken out of it. We have to try and judge without being judgemental, to disagree without moralising.

If your child lies to you, the first thing to do is to normalise it. It is just a lie, let's not get carried away with the whole moral issue of lying, the hurt you may feel that your child has done this, and the whys and wherefores of telling lies.

Kids sometimes tell lies. That's what kids do. It is often just glorified storytelling that may get a bit out of hand. If you were to question them about it, they may well not be sure they were telling stories. Sometimes the truth and imagination just become a bit mixed up. We all want our nearest and dearest to think well of us, so sometimes we tell a bit of a story and then, because of the way they behave, it might get a bit more complicated and a bit deeper until we suddenly find that we cannot easily get out of it without losing face. It is not always about you and how you have been with the child in the past, it is often just about them and what they think your expectations of them might be.

This telling of stories, stretching the truth, or actually telling big lies can be an important part of learning about the idea of not telling lies. First, you need to put on the coat of somebody who is not truthful. You need to live in it for a while. You will deal with the consequences of what you have said and then you will, hopefully, come around to thinking about the fact that, all in all, you prefer to be somebody who tells the truth.

Children are children and they need to be that way. We have to understand them and be ready to accept the things they sometimes do and say with good humour and understanding, and most especially, without rushing off in a panic and thinking that they are blighted for life or in need of some kind of professional help.

Only the other day, I had an email from a parent whose son is at Summerhill. She was seriously worried because her child had said that somebody had broken one of his valuable belongings and nothing had been done about it. Upon looking into this, we found that nobody had broken this item and that the boy had accidentally broken it himself. I did not investigate the reason he had said this because it does not really matter. He made something up, he will feel a bit bad about it, but it will have been an excellent learning experience and will last him a lifetime.

A common one will be whether the child has been going to classes or not. Children, feeling an expectation from their parents, will sometimes make up reasons why they are not going. The lessons are too easy, they are not interesting, I am with a group of children who are not as advanced as me ...

It is a difficult thing to tell a parent that their child has lied to them. It's a bit akin to telling somebody that they are making a mess of being parents — absolute taboo to most people.

Usually, I will get a reply saying: 'Oh dear, it was clearly a mistake, but everything seems to be fine', and sometimes I will get a reply asking how dare I suggest that this child would lie to their mother or father as they have always been so open and honest with one another.

But it is not about honesty; it is about growing and learning and making mistakes. It needs careful handling, and whatever happens or is said, it must never humiliate the child. I would always go for not saying anything at all if possible. If there is no need to go into it, then I would not. It is essential that we do not break a trust or humiliate a child by 'catching them out'. It is better to leave it until sometime, often much later when you can just drop in the fact that you knew all along and it was no big deal at all. Sometimes being that surprising grown-up gives you a whole lot of other respect!

There was a lovely advert for washing powder that made me smile. A young man is bringing his filthy clothes home for his mum to wash for him after going to the Glastonbury music festival or somewhere like it. She is chastising him a bit for the mess, and he remarks how she probably did the same thing when she was young.

She smiles a bit wickedly and says: 'Yes, we probably did, but we did not bring any dirty clothes home to be washed because when we were young, we didn't WEAR any clothes!'

Then a lovely shot of him giving her a double-take with a shocked expression and her just looking totally serious and innocent because in those heady days at pop festivals in the 1960s, of course, we often took our clothes off!

Occasionally children do not learn by the mistakes they make in this way. Some children have very many reasons why they will lie or cheat or bully. This, in my mind, comes under emotional unhappiness and will need some more serious attention to help it on its way. At Summerhill, we give the children the freedom to find their way as much as possible amid the structure and democratic process of the school Meetings and the Ombudsmen system while still following their own path as people. It can be a bit of a journey but generally, left alone to make their own choices; they learn what is acceptable behaviour when living with other people, so it comes right in the end.

Playing, talking to friends, spending time with adults who are calm and not too personally involved, all of these things contribute to assisting in the healing process, unbeknown to the child at the time. Perhaps at home, the extended family or trusted family friends can help give that perspective and a less intense emotional connection than with their parents, their closest loved ones.

When professionals are rehabilitating wild creatures or abused animals, they use the technique of 'advance and retreat' where you put on a bit of pressure (advance) and then quickly remove it again (retreat) so that the animal can learn to trust that you will not invade their space.

We notice that a lot of new pupils will get on their bikes and spend many hours just cycling around our school grounds, up and down hills, around the clay hump, round and round the house, almost as though they are cycling away from their old lives and into the new. It gives them time to watch and assimilate this new situation while being engaged in their own activity. This is something that we can all learn from, the idea of giving people a place — and space — and a role (in this case, riding the bicycle) to let themselves gradually slip into a new situation.

I keep on mentioning animal training and I make no apology for it. Closely watching wild or domesticated animals is hugely rewarding and also tells us a great deal about ourselves, human beings. Animals react instinctively and I have observed that children do too; in fact, we all do to some degree, but as we grow up, we become 'thinkers' rather than 'feelers', whereas children remain emotional and perceptive.

We humans have taken millions of years to reach our so-called civilised state, and a lot of the instincts that we relied on seem to have been lost, but of course, they have not really. I think we need to learn to listen to them more, just plain old instincts that tell you whether you should jump off that high rock or not (and then don't jump off, of course!).

It is not easy in daily family life at home to provide an environment like Summerhill for your child, to be able to take the pressure off what is, by necessity, a conventional school life. So, what can we do?

Remain on the side of the child. Talk about how daft the education system can be, if that is what you think, and how limited it is in reaching and really engaging with the whole child. Always take the side of your child on the issue of too much homework or test results.

Although most parents are not able to change schools or do home-schooling, there are many things in your whole attitude to school that can help your child cope with it, knowing they are not on their own in their opinions and doubts important.

Last but not least, try to give them masses of time at home where they have no pressure to do anything other than be a child and enjoy playing in whatever form that might take, be it running through the garden with a bow and arrow or socialising with friends.

Computers and gaming

Gaming isn't all evil. It can also be a very social activity. Kids interact with each other often when playing. They also learn many skills such as reading, strategies and writing on a keyboard.

So, best not to totally demonise gaming or computer use. Our school rules are unambiguous. No screen use for entertainment between 9 am and 4 pm on weekdays and not after bedtime.

If you are caught, you get a screen ban for usually 24 hours but up to 48 hours. If you break screen bans, it comes to the Meeting, and as a rule, devices are temporarily confiscated. On the whole this all works very well. We have elected 'Screening Police' who can fine 'on the spot' (without bringing it to the Meeting). Any case of a person persistently screening is likely to come to the Meeting. There have been times when a particular person has been discussed in the Meeting as their peers had concerns about the amount of screening they do. Sometimes pupils propose that they are an exception to this rule and if they give a good reason it might be carried.

Interesting to see how many grownups, when challenged, do actually admit that they use devices far too often, so parents need to lead by example. If you are constantly reaching for your phone, even for business purposes, it is not only rude in front of other people, but it is a bad example to children and you certainly cannot enforce rules that you are not going to adhere to yourself. If it is not already in place, families might consider a complete ban on all screens at family eating times.

Sometimes parents tell us that their child is addicted to gaming. First of all, I think one has to be very careful about using the word 'addiction'. Addiction is a serious condition where a person becomes completely dependent upon something to the exclusion of a normal life and usually with very dire consequences. Many, many children get involved in playing computer games and using devices so that they seem to be taking over — but this is absolutely not addiction. By using this word, you immediately imply that the person is unable to stop what they are doing, which turns them into a victim and exonerates them of any responsibility to break the chain.

I have played computer games years ago when they were on consoles, but no less exciting. The first thing you learn is that time flies when you are playing. So maybe a tight timetable seems very unfair to the player as you no sooner get going than you have to stop. Maybe make longer periods (as we do at school) but less often. Getting down to an honest discussion about what will work better for both parties is a good idea.

Probably there will have to be some strict rules, particularly at the start.

I would certainly put some constraints upon a child living in my house in this modern age. We have to remember that the people who create computer programmes are highly paid parts of the vast multinational business that specialises in making what they offer as persuasive as possible. It is in their interest to do so. We must bear in mind that there is no way that a child can be expected to ration themselves sufficiently when put against the might of the computer gaming companies and their persuasive games. They need our help and sympathy, but also our honesty and strength.

Working out what is going to be the best plan should be guided by the child as well. Yes, I would advise parents sticking to their guns and not allowing free access to screening, but also they need to listen to the other party and be prepared to negotiate.

As mentioned earlier, perhaps at weekends on Friday evening, Saturday and Sunday until bedtime would be fair maybe in the school holidays a week or so of complete freedom to game all and every day. Something like that. Remember that the school term is really taxing for children in many ways, even just being out there and socialising, getting up in the mornings, having a timetable. It is nice to be able to completely chill and just do whatever you want for a while.

I don't think that computer games or screening are the enemy, but they do need to be kept in check. We say that the dog should be wagging its tail, rather than the tail wagging the dog!

Another word about the use of computers and gaming at home: A parent some years ago contacted me to say that her son, then around fourteen years old, was playing computers in his room almost all holidays and she was worried. I shared this with the staff when we got back to the new term and the feedback I got was that he was very diligent about the school computer laws, not going online out of hours at all. He said that in the holidays — his holidays too, of course — he enjoyed being able to play as much as he liked! He is now a young adult at university studying — guess what — computing. A thoroughly well balanced and impressive young man!

Try not to forget that the school holidays are your child's holidays too — and that might mean eating too much chocolate, as we all do on holiday, and wanting to crash out, sleep late and play too much computer. A compromise about how the holiday time is worked should consider this fact, that it is the child's holiday and they will feel that they have been working really hard at school all term and now might like and need a break, something that I think parents often forget.

Remember — your holidays are your child's holidays too.
That might mean them crashing out and sleeping late.

It is often the grown-ups who are busy thinking about all the 'fun' things they will do together during the holidays, not actually looking at it from the child's point of view. Sometimes just chilling on your own is what you need after a busy term immersed among other people at school. Another element of this is that sitting quietly playing computer games can be a very good physical and mental break, especially around exam time.

Personally, I would not get too anxious about it in the holidays and would not even try to curtail their gaming very much. I would try to bear in mind that my ideal holiday with the children, spending lots of fun time together, may not be their perfect holiday. For them, maybe spending a lot of time sleeping and gaming gives them that special holiday feeling. It reminds us that it is always good to look at childhood from outside the box and try to see it from a completely different angle. We tend to imagine that our children must be thinking as we do, and they do not. Good old negotiation and compromise is probably the best thing. A week or so of gaming and a week or so of family outings ...

Teenage anxiety and depression

Emotional anxiety or stress about emotional anxiety is intruding more and more into the lives of our young people. While it is excellent that society is taking mental illness more seriously, we are, at the same time, unwittingly creating a generation of young people convinced that they may have mental health problems. I do not think that this is a healthy state of affairs at all. At Summerhill, our approach to teenage difficulties is much more laid back than most modern parents.

Somehow natural emotions and emotional responses are getting lost amongst all the anxiety. People talk about having a mental health problem because they have recently lost a mother, father or friend instead of recognising that the misery, the sadness, the wretchedness are all normal responses. Looking at the way the media and social media work and manipulate our feelings, it seems as though the human race constantly hopes it can live a life without any pain or suffering at all. As though it should all be pink unicorns and fluffy rabbits. If this does not happen, then there must surely be something wrong with us, we must be failures.

I believe that if you mistake these normal feelings for mental health problems, then it can put you into a box. You become a person who is unwell, mentally ill. I do not think this can be helpful to anybody, 'I am a person with a mental health problem', instead of 'I am having a tough time at the moment' are very different statements. I am just not sure how helpful being in the box is.

In reality, if a person is grieving deeply for whatever reason, it may be — either a tragedy in the family or their doubts and uncertainties, then, of course, they are emotionally unbalanced and upset. It is called mourning and is a very natural response to a tragedy. We can get through it. We may need somebody to talk to about it, often that extended family or close friend, but it is normal and not a mental illness.

We do our young people a great injustice if we lead them down the path of having a mental 'condition' when they are suffering emotionally over things that are very clear to see and understand. It disempowers them, removes their autonomy and in a way infantilises them. I have watched this happen many times. I have seen strong, assertive, confident young people turn into weak unhappy souls who feel that they cannot manage to work out their problems without considerable support or even medication.

I know that support is important, very important, but at the end of the day, I think it better for a young person to feel that they are going through a 'bad patch' which is transient and will soon be over than to go along the path of calling it a mental health problem. Until we can all redefine our attitude to the name 'mental health problem', it will continue to bring connotations of somebody who has lost their mind somehow and is unable to manage life for themselves.

Just as we believe in giving children the freedom to learn about themselves, so it goes without saying that at Summerhill, we feel the amount of intervention provided for young people is very often not appropriate and can, in fact, be detrimental. Our first line will always be that our pupils are ordinary young people going through all the trials and tribulations that all young people go through.

Giving them the label of being 'depressed' or 'special' is the same thing to us as labelling conditions such as ADHD, Asperger's, etc. Clinical labels can help give medical information, but that is not the major story here. Labels begin to define the young person both in their own eyes and the eyes of those around them. Just because a young person says that they feel mixed up, confused, depressed does not mean that these terms should define them. Many of the above feelings are part of growing up and need to be seen in perspective. We must not allow our young people to mistake sadness and uncertainty for mental health issues.

I would say, controversially, that we do not feel the need to recognise this condition called ADHD at all formally. Yes, we see many very individual young people — and we rejoice in that individuality, but they are perfectly normal and quickly learn to live in our community in harmony with themselves and all of us.

I cannot do maths. I know that if I went to see somebody, they would diagnose some reason why this is the case, something to do with the way my brain works (or does not work!). Actually, I do not care. How is it going to enhance my life? I already know that I cannot do maths, I just put my hands up and say: 'I can't do maths', I am fine with it, always have been, never had a problem with it even as a child. I believe this is due to the environment that I was brought up in, where I was allowed to feel pride in myself for the things that I could do and not ashamed of the things that I could not do.

I recognise that a diagnosis (and a label) has been helpful for some people, particularly in the environment that most of us have to live in. Chris Packham, the Naturalist, for example, has found great strength in his diagnosis of Asperger's and it has obviously helped him towards where he is now as a person. I commend him for it.

I would probably argue the point with him that if he had had the environment of somewhere like Summerhill, then he would not have needed this diagnosis. I would certainly never judge him or look at him as a person with Asperger's. I would judge him just as Chris, the man I meet. But this discussion is reserved for the day that he and I share a cup of coffee and a chat!

There is absolutely nothing wrong with an adult seeking to discover why they may have always had an aversion to maths or science or writing if it helps them to assimilate things by knowing that they have some sort of condition. But let us encourage our youngsters to wait until they are older and living as adults, just as one would do with something huge like the issue of gender alteration. This is not something that children need to be thinking about when they should be learning about themselves and those around them; there is time enough for all of it in the future if that is what an individual feels that they need.

On the subject of labelling, somebody tweeted me the other day because I had been saying that if we stopped putting children in stressful situations, we would probably not need to use labelling; after all, they would not display symptoms that would require a label.

This person said, 'Let me have a label if I want one'.

I am not saying that you should not have a label; I am not saying there should be no labels, and I am not saying there are no existing conditions. What I am saying is that I do not think we should be labelling children because of the failure of our education systems. If you are 18, past the age of consent, or preferably in your twenties and you feel that a label will help you, then go for it!

But from what I have seen at Summerhill, labelling is more often a negative thing and not a positive one. This is not open for argument; it is just a fact as we see it every day. As I have said in an earlier paragraph, I can absolutely understand why parents feel the need to go down that route when their child is getting a hard time at school, and a label might bring about a difference.

Sadly, the education systems throughout most of the world are only designed to teach subjects and information, not to allow emotional growth to a great degree. So although most schools do work hard to try and offer a 'broad and balanced curriculum', regrettably, the very system itself does not make it possible. Most of the time, children are given a label to explain why they are not conforming to the system's expectations or are reacting negatively to life in general and school in particular. In effect, we are providing a system of education that is helping to damage our children and then looking for answers and applying all sorts of sticking plasters to try and solve the problem, when we should be looking at the situation in the first place.

Our education system has never really been thought out — it has evolved over many years in answer to a set of problems that were different to the issues of today and has not been upgraded to any radical degree since its inception.

My father wrote in his first book about the madness of teaching bairns in his small Scottish school all sorts of things that they were never going to need or use throughout their lives and doing so to the real detriment of their emotions and childhood happiness. These bairns were destined to be farmers and labourers, and he felt that wielding the 'tawse' to punish them for not learning subjects that had no real relevance to their lives was a cruel thing to do.

A. S. Neill wrote:
'The function of the child is to live his own life — not the life that his anxious parents think he should live, nor the life according to the purpose of the educator who thinks he knows best'.

The critical point is that no child should be bullied or traumatised into learning what we adults think they ought to learn, and this applies as much, if not more so, today than ever. We know so much more about psychology and the negative effects of stress and trauma; we are much less accepting of inhumane treatment of individuals and yet it still goes on.

A. S. Neill wrote:
'I have converted a hard-working school into a playground, and I rejoice. These bairns have had a year of happiness and liberty. They have done what they liked; they have sung their songs while they were working at graphs, they have eaten their sweets while they read their books, they have hung on my arms as we rambled along in search of artistic corners.'

He wrote this while working in Gretna Green school in 1914. This experience for Neill was the very beginning of Summerhill ...

Things have changed. Our society is not accepting a lot of the things that were accepted even 30 years ago. Children are now more confident about defying things that they were afraid to react to many years ago. Take the environmental marches, for example. This means that often children are getting more and more challenging to deal with in school situations when they are not happy.

The pressure to achieve, and the expectations of adults and society, have now taken over from the threat of a beating at school. It might seem more humane, but to some children, it can be just as deadly. Remember that although many children find schoolwork easy and who enjoy the praise they receive and the sense of achievement, there are many more who do not find it easy, who struggle every day, not only to understand the work required but also to pay attention to subjects in which they have no natural interest. These children perceive that they are stupid, not as clever as everybody else. Even if they do not display symptoms of emotional stress, what they are learning every day is this: 'I am a failure, I am struggling to do what everybody else seems to find easy.'

What a burden to carry into your adult life, being a failure for something that is entirely not your fault. Naturally, you are not really a failure; there is no such thing as a failure. We can all fail at certain things. I am quite sure that I could never be a good mountaineer — I am afraid of heights.

My husband Tony met a young woman some years ago who had been the class star in their old Grammar school. She had worked hard, been a bit of a swat and kindly had helped him with his homework (well, actually, she did most of it for him!). He praised her for this and asked how she was getting along in life. She has a good job in the city and seems happy enough, but she told Tony that she had hated every day of school and was terrified most of the time too.

The idea of failure at school is only because you may have skills and interests that were not catered for in your particular school. It is the education system that has failed you.

This quote is attributed to Albert Einstein:
'Everybody is a genius. But if you judge a fish by its ability to climb a tree, it will live its whole life believing that it is stupid.'

And here is a quote from Neill that we have put into our General Policy Statement:

'Learning is important — but not to everyone. Nijinsky could not pass his school exams in St. Petersburg, and he could not enter the State Ballet without passing those exams. He simply could not learn school subjects — his mind was elsewhere. They faked an exam for him, giving him the answers with the papers — so a biography says. What a loss to the world if Nijinsky had really to pass those exams!'

I am not here to criticise or judge the prevailing education systems of the world, but I can say that there is a lot of evidence to show that these systems are harmful to many children. What a shame that those with the power to create change in this area seem to be blind to the possibilities.

It all seems so simple — if you force children into situations that they find too challenging, too difficult, too boring or too stressful, then it will create a reaction in them. More often than not, this reaction is to either withdraw and become unhappy and anxious. If the child is of a different temperament, it can manifest itself as a trouble maker, a live wire, a rebel who disrupts the classroom, and often the home as well.

So, we look for a problem, find one, label it and then think that we have got it solved, but of course, we have not. It will be a very long road to solve and may not be unravelled by the end.

If society treated any other group of people the way it treats its children there would be an outcry. It would be seen as serious prejudice and would probably raise questions about human rights. But as they are children and we have a traditional view of how we can control children, then it seems that society is comfortable with what we do and the incredibly negative results that can be the outcome.

So, why do we not give those children the time and space to manage their own learning, their own playing, their own lives to a degree? Take away the boredom, the pressure, the fear and let them enjoy a happy childhood in which they feel valued players who have some real control over what happens. Very often, these negative feelings in the child are a direct result of not being heard.

We had a boy at Summerhill who had been diagnosed with ADHD. One day his mother turned to me and said, with tears in her eyes:

'I had to go down that route of getting him diagnosed. He was getting detentions every day and life was a real misery for him. Once he was diagnosed, then he had less pressure and more respect was paid to him.'

Of course, I would not blame a mother for that — but I do blame the system that did not hear that child's silent pleas, nor see his pain, and did not find the obvious answer which was to allow him to express some of his natural exuberance in ways that would not cause problems for teachers and classmates.

So many times I have watched professional people with many years of training and experience talking to children and asking them all the right questions about how they feel, what they would like, how could they solve their problems? And then I watch, in astonishment, when they do not take any action at all.

So a child might say that they do not want any more assessments with the Educational Psychologist, everybody will nod their heads and pay lip service to that, but the truth is that they will still have those sessions because that is what the professionals think is best for them. You cannot gain the trust and respect of young people if you are not prepared to listen and act upon what they say. I have seen a number of young people being cajoled and persuaded to remain on medication even though they were fighting against the whole idea; actually, there was no real choice in the first place for these youngsters.

Many great teachers who are in the role for all the right reasons, could if they were not hampered by a fundamentally flawed system, help their pupils fly as high as the sky. It could be a wonderful outcome with creative learning and emotional development — and as much academic work as each individual felt was right for them with no pressure to conform, no expectations, and no anxiety about what a child will develop into if we adults do not control their lives at every step. We just need an acceptance that we are all individuals and will not all be high flyers in finance, doctors or lawyers, or great scientists. Some of us will be happy to do more mundane things in the world, and we can all be outstanding at what we do and take tremendous pleasure in it!

We all know that taking pleasure in your work makes you much better at that particular job. An old Summerhill pupil once said to me, talking about the experience he had with his learning and how it had not robbed him of his love for it: 'When you are on a flight to New York from Heathrow in a jumbo jet — what you really want to know is that the person flying that plane just LOVES THEIR JOB!'

As parents and citizens, we should not just lie down and let this continue to happen. Our school system is causing colossal grief and unhappiness to many of our children, and we should be out on the streets with banners — shouting, nay, screaming that this is not good enough and that it must change!

Don't try to make life perfect

First of all, 'perfect' is impossible to achieve. Life is life. There are great and lovely things and there are really awful things. Showering children with possessions, holidays, and outings whilst trying to shield them from reality is not just a bad idea; I believe it is seriously damaging. One of the things I tell prospective parents about Summerhill is that children will need to learn to live with others on an equal basis. They will learn about communication, negotiation and compromise, three of the fundamentals we all need in life.

The way they will learn this is simple. In an average household the adults are pretty easy to live with in one respect — for instance, when there is cake for tea and the child wants the first or the largest slice, they can usually get it. Why? Because grown-ups aren't that interested, they don't care very much whether they get the biggest portion of cake. But at Summerhill, there will be around 70 other children living with you who will all want that biggest piece, and your child will have to learn that sometimes, no matter how much you wish for it, you don't always get what you want!

Talking about shielding from reality, our youngest son, Neill, at the age of four, was cast into a huge tragedy and sadness when one of our Summerhill pupils did not return to school one Autumn term because he had a severe asthma attack. Akira subsequently died, and the whole school, including all of our family, were cast into deep mourning. Akira had been here since he was six and was now almost fourteen. He had been the best friend of Neill's older brother, Henry who was, naturally, broken-hearted and struggled to deal with the situation.

I cannot imagine how it must have been for our little Neill, at that tender age, watching everything unfold as we all grieved, but he came through it just fine. A couple of years later his much-loved grandmother died, and a couple of years after that, his other one died. This was a lot for a little lad to deal with, and the reason I relate it is because it was real life, it happened, and through the honesty of feeling, love and laughter, we all got through it. It is part of who we all are, and Neill, in particular, has grown into who he is because of it. You cannot shield children from some of the terrible things that happen and if you try, I believe you do them a great disservice.

We all get it wrong sometimes

Somebody told me about their friends who follow a 'child-led' philosophy in bringing up their children. He said that, for instance, when they go to the beach, they tend to follow the child around rather than ask him to follow them or do what they want to do. My first thought was: 'Why not just leave the child alone and sit in the sunshine while he wanders around and does his own thing?'

One starry night my father went for a walk with his friend, the philosopher Bertrand Russell. 'Russell', he said, 'the difference between us is this; if we had a child with us now, you would be telling him all about the stars, while I would stay quiet and leave him with his own thoughts.'

This sums up exactly what I mean about child-led. Yes, let it be a child-led family, but please don't do any following! And be oh-so-careful that 'child-led' does not turn into a life that is 'child-controlled'.

Neill's famous story about the grand piano comes to mind. Neill was interviewing a parent who was going on about how wonderful his books were and how much she admired his work.

'Mr Neill,' she said, 'I have read all your books and have raised my daughter exactly following your methods.' Her daughter was standing on his grand piano with her dirty boots and then took a great leap for the sofa and nearly went through the springs. 'See how natural she is,' said the mother. 'The perfect Neillian child!' Neill didn't say anything at the time though he commented later that he disagreed strongly with the mother.

This is an illustration of how people can, and very often do, get it wrong. I cannot count the number of times I have talked with parents whose children were having big problems communicating with and living harmoniously with other people. They are nodding and saying yes to everything I am advising them to do as though they have been doing it all the time.

Getting child-rearing wrong is not a crime. It is a whole big thing in our lives that needs to be learned and constantly juggled about until we get it right.

Very often, our children are a mirror of how we are doing as parents. I think it is crucial to reassess things to make sure that we are getting it right. If our children are very hyper, argumentative, sulky and demanding, they could have ADHD or something similar or, on the other hand, they could just be like that because our system at home has some flaws. It is always good to have little reassessments and think about having a change of direction. There is no shame in suddenly deciding that you have been getting things wrong. Just be aware that any radical changes will take a while to run smoothly. Give it time and take it steadily.

It is never too late to make changes, to talk to your children and, yes, maybe to apologise for past attitudes and actions if you feel that you need to.

I think that most children suffer hugely from the fact that they feel not in control of their lives and their own destiny.

An interesting survey in the UK by UNICEF (2018) showed that a third of children feel that they are not being listened to or asked to share their input on family decisions. Now, one could argue that the adults should run the family as they are the ones who know best. But in a world where more and more minority groups can express their views, it goes without saying that children will have those expectations and want to have their opinions taken seriously. In Summerhill, we have been doing this for 100 years, so it is not a difficult thing for us. It already has a long-standing history and grounding to enable it to happen effectively and encourage and help children learn how to manage this issue of taking responsibility for their actions.

We have to tread a fine line between giving a child freedom to be in control of their lives while still being able to live in harmony with others and without becoming the proverbial 'spoiled brat'; earlier in the book I wrote about 'Freedom not Licence'. Being in control of your life absolutely does not mean having your own way all the time. It means being a valued participant in life decisions about things that are relevant to you. This is as relevant in families as it is elsewhere.

For younger children, it means not being nagged at all the time about what they can and cannot do. It means being allowed to find their own way and make mistakes. For older children, it means being able to feel that they can approach adults and talk about such issues as school work, exam preparation, sex or life choices and that there will be no expectations of them. I really mean, no expectations at all.

Giving your child freedom to live their own life means freedom to be the person they feel they want to be, even if this means that they do not want to take the route through school and university that you and the wider family and friends would want or expect them to take. It means being prepared to support them through the decisions they make, good or bad, and if that means going against their school, or your father-in-law or anyone else, then so be it.

Naturally, you can, and should, express yourself about the situation if you want to. If you think your child is unrealistic to want to be a vet when they hate animals and science, that's fine. But you approach it just as you would if your best friend was making such a life decision. You should try to wield no more power than that, and if you do not take such a polite and advisory role, it will create anger, frustration and rebellion, not to mention a lot of unhappiness and feelings of betrayal. Remember, you must be unquestionably on the side of the child at all times, even when they are wrong, and you are angry!

If things in family life feel as though they are tumbling downhill out of control, then it might be time for that reassessment and some serious thought about the future and how you want your relationship with the children. As I said earlier, it might also be time to reassess yourself and why you are possibly finding some things difficult. It is vital that we do not bring our own neuroses and anxieties into the home situation. A healthy dose of self-criticism might be the order of the day; how much of this is about me and not about the children at all? How much of it comes from my own background and the fact that I had expectations put upon me? How much from fear of not fitting the 'norm' in society?

It is essential to understand that 'having some issues' about things does not mean that you are crazy. We are all developments of both nurture and nature. The personality traits that you carry will respond differently to the way other people's traits will respond. Take three people and put them through the same family, and they will all come out differently; sometimes it is obvious why 'she was always such a live-wire' or 'he was always very quiet and studious', but at other times it is an absolute enigma!

As parents, we need to stop beating ourselves up about what we may have done wrong and simply say: 'Yes, I got it wrong, this is all new to me, and I don't know how to do it'. You can turn it around and try something different. Give it a really good try, give it time and see what difference it makes to your life and that of your child. Is it at all possible to take time out, away from the family situation?

I think that sometimes being able to take a few days away, on your own, to somewhere beautiful, can be an excellent time to clear your thoughts and come back refreshed.

Don't panic!

Everybody knows how difficult children can be; toddler tantrums, demanding 11-year olds, teenage rebels. But what people don't realise is that the adults bring about many of the difficulties themselves through the way children are traditionally managed in our society.

Take toddlers, for example. Our domestic pattern is to teach infants from the beginning about obedience, manners and response to danger. Due to their self-centred needs, little children have no comprehension of what 'thank you' represents at all. It is a bit like asking them to understand the theory behind algebra. If a person is not emotionally ready to accept or understand an idea, it is a complete waste of time trying to achieve it. And why do we need our children to say 'Thank you' anyway? Is it to try and improve how we might be seen as parents — 'We have a polite little child saying thank you'?

At Summerhill, we feel that the sentiment behind a statement is the most important thing. We do not encourage kids to say 'sorry' when they are brought up in the school Meetings; in fact, we steer away from it. 'Sorry' is better shown by the way you attempt not to do it again or show some understanding of what you have done. The words themselves can be quite meaningless.

How can we teach anything if the recipient does not understand what we are trying to teach? Take a two-year-old. There is a coffee table with a lovely big ornament on it. Naturally, the child wants to look at the ornament, but what do we do? We say 'no'. We may take the child's hand away as well. Now, what reason would a toddler understand why we are doing this? From her point of view, it is totally illogical. She sees the object, it interests her, so she wants to look at it. If we say no, it becomes more fascinating and more likely that she will touch it and probably knock it over or drop it when your head is turned. So what is wrong with allowing her to handle it in the first place? Let her look at it, with help if it is fragile until her curiosity is satisfied, then either return it to the table or, preferably, put it away temporarily until she is older.

If children are given this type of respect from the beginning, it is rare for something to get broken, as they are usually very careful; it is children who are constantly told 'NO' who are tense, anxious and more likely to break things.

This applies to the danger element as well. Telling a child from their earliest days to 'be careful', 'don't touch it', 'come away from there' has the same effect as the table ornament. There is no logic in it for the child, plus the fact that many, many parents just continue to say it over

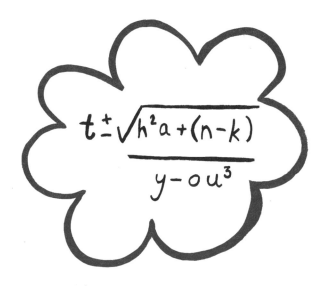

Little children do not understand what 'Thank you' means.

and over again until, after a short while, the child ignores it.

Like the two dogs who are chatting as they trot across the park. One dog says to the other: 'What's your name?'. 'I dunno', says the first dog, 'but I think it might be "NO, Naughty Dog!"'

As an adult, who would you listen to the most? Is it the person who keeps shouting at you and warning you not to try anything, do anything, risk anything; or is it the person who watches you take risks, is there for you when you need them and occasionally steps in to tell you that what you are about to do is absolutely not a good idea at all?

A constant stream of warnings and orders only teaches children one thing — to ignore them. Sure, you can teach them to obey by shouting or smacking, but it doesn't last, does it? Sadly, it is still legal for parents to smack their children in England, Wales and Northern Ireland (though in 2022, Wales was due to follow Scotland, where hitting your child is now illegal). Children get used to shouting and to being hit as well. You cannot trust somebody who is bullied into submission, and what happens when the smacks don't work anymore — more violence?

A friend of mine was in a butcher's shop one day recently. There was a freezer with some sausages and so-on in it. It had no lid. A little boy was casually dropping sawdust from the floor into the freezer. The mother, intent upon her shopping with the butcher, kept shouting to him: 'Craig, stop it Craig. Leave it alone'. The boy continued without a second glance back at his mum.

My worry is what sort of an adult is young Craig going to become after what he learned in the butcher's shop on that day. Fundamentally, I can do whatever I want. My mother will tell me not to, but I can just keep on doing it anyway.

That is a dangerous thing to learn about yourself. Hopefully, young Craig will have found some other boundaries in his life that he respected enough to help keep himself and those around him safe.

Do they think what we think they think?

Looking at life through the child's eyes can be very difficult. We all have views and thoughts about what our children are or ought to be, and quite often, this is not a true picture. We tell parents at Summerhill that we generally see a very different child at school to the one that they see at home. I think this is because the child you see at home is often the one that you expect to see or that they want you to see. We have spoken before about the way that children, because they love you so much, want to appear perfect for you.

We need to stop and look again at our children and the people we think they are and face reality if we find they were not what we thought they were.

There was a lovely joke going around on the Internet that showed pictures of things that people think and the reality of what is actually happening. The one I am thinking of is about massage — it says:

'*What my friends think I do*' and shows a picture of many hands gently rubbing somebody's back; the next is:
'*What my parents think I do*' with a picture of a hippy.
'*What society thinks I do*' — a picture of a very obvious prostitute chatting to a customer.
'*What doctors think I do*'– a picture of an old-world medicine man.
'*What I think I do*', a picture of a glorious light shining down from above and changing the world.
'*What I really do*', a picture of somebody looking harassed and busy handwashing a whole lot of sheets and couch covers!

This is a fun joke, but it actually shows a relevant point — what we want or think and what our children want or think, are very often very different.

So my joke would be:
'*What we think our children want to do in the holidays*', with a picture of a family having a happy time together at the seaside playing on the beach.
'*What our children really want to do in the holidays*', with a picture of somebody sleeping late in the morning and getting up to play computer games and eat trashy food with their pyjamas on.

I know that is an extreme kind of joke, but I am sure you get the point.
When my grandchildren were little and early pupils at Summerhill,

I would watch them, at the age of five, standing in the queue for their meals, taking the knife and fork out of the box, choosing where to sit and then eating their lunch or supper all by themselves. When we had a family meal, I used to laugh with my daughter Amy as she called to those same grandchildren to come and choose what they wanted, helped them by serving the food onto the plate and then carried it to the table for them. She was aware of what she was doing, and it was a bit of a family joke. She said (tongue in cheek) that she was trying to keep them little and be dependent upon her for as long as possible, and we needed to indulge her in that! So we did, and they went back to school each term and were once again those independent little folk who perfectly happily managed their own lives.

Children are not trying to constantly climb to the top of the pecking order in the same way many animal species need to do. You do not have to keep proving your authority over them in case they become uncontrollable. Children are people, and, as with all of us, they respond to being treated with respect, love and approval.

In past times it was common for parents to think that babies had to be left to cry because if you were seen to 'give in to them' then they would become demanding children and adults. There were 'just trying to get their own way'. This has been an underlying problem in child rearing for many years, and it needs to be filed away in the rubbish compartment. Children are not that devious or cunning. They are natural little creatures that respond to their normal desires and inner programming, which is born into all humans and most animals — that of wanting to play and be joyous in life, learn and discover, love and care.

Some important points for parents

Treat your children with the kind of respect that you would show an adult and as you would like to be respected yourself. Have the same expectations the other way around, particularly of how they will respectfully treat you.

Be quick to analyse yourself and recognise your own fears, desires, and prejudices to ensure that you give your children honesty and openness and that you are not projecting your problems onto them. I have already written about your preparation as a parent; assessing your ability to be a good parent and overcoming issues you feel may hinder this process is what you need to do. I have seen very many children struggle with substantial emotional problems caused by a mother or father's anxiety about them directly due to the parent's fears, anger or insecurity about their own lives. To be honest, until that parent can put their hands up and accept their part in the problem, it is impossible to solve until, probably, well into adulthood.

Love your children unreservedly and show them that you love them, whatever they do. Be their champion in all circumstances. But be sure to see the reality of who they are and what they may have done wrong. Putting your head in the sand is destructive to the extreme. If your child is a bully, you really need to face up to that and be prepared while giving them all the love in the world to tell them that they are absolutely out of order and deplore what they are doing. Never be too proud or naive to see that your child might just be trying to display things in a different light to you than what is the reality. Children can tell lies. It happens sometimes!

Give them the freedom to be themselves and understand that children need to be children, be silly, make noise and mess, argue amongst themselves, and be childish. Be sure to expect that they respect your rights too and cherish your own right to freedom. This means that they must understand when you need some quiet time or that you like to keep things tidy. They can go and play somewhere else if they want to make noise or leave a mess.

Allow them to make their own mistakes. We adults cannot always make sure that life is good or right for them. Sometimes they need to learn from their own mistakes.

Be honest, tell the truth, don't be afraid to discuss things about life in front of or with them. Children can deal with many awful things. It does not 'rob them of their childhood'. Give them the respect that allows them to feel strong feelings of joy and sorrow, laughter or disgust and let them know about the nastier side of what happens in the world. But of course, always ensure that this is age-appropriate. You might discuss Female Genital Mutilation with a teenager, but of course, not talk about it in front of a seven-year-old.

Remember that the needs of children and adults are very different. Adults usually like a tidy home, whereas children can live in a rubbish tip without ever noticing it! If you are not understanding of this and have expectations, it will only cause conflict. This probably means that, for now, you will have to tidy up their rooms for them. It won't spoil them. They will want (or at least be able) to do it themselves by the time they are in their mid-teens, and by the time they have their own families, they will probably have spotless homes!

Try to find your inner child and be prepared to play infantile games sometimes, giggle at silly things, and be human. Try not always to be the sensible adult, but at the same time definitely do not try to behave like a child to impress them or be 'one of the gang'. It will look false, and your children will find it embarrassing to the extreme.

Try not to have expectations of who they will become. You cannot decide whether they will be a road sweeper, a great surgeon or an opera star. Support them in their interests, try not to let schoolwork get them down or put them under pressure. Let them know that you support them, even against their school, if it is necessary.

There need to be firm boundaries in the family home, 'Freedom not Licence' we say at Summerhill. If you think that bedtime should be at a specific time, then set it; that is fine, but make sure the children have a voice too, that they feel they can talk to you or get angry with you sometimes. Maybe, with the question of bedtimes for older children, you could make some compromises as we do at Summerhill by allowing late nights on Friday and Saturdays so that the children can feel empowered and have some control. Things that matter particularly to them are very important. In your home, you need to be in charge; the children must know that you are there to keep the family running safely, that you will make decisions and look after them, but within this, they must have the freedom to be themselves as well. Children very often feel insecure and anxious if their parents are not in control or if the boundaries are fuzzy.

Leadership is a word that I do not like very much for the connotations it implies. However, for want of a better one, I will use it. All children need some kind of guidance, help, leadership, call it what you may. I think a good illustration of the type of leadership I am talking about might be when somebody has invited you to stay in their house. The person you are visiting is in charge and you are comfortable knowing that. You want to feel safe in their home, that they know what they are doing. They decide which room you will sleep in; they make the food, set the mealtimes, change the bed linen and might often plan some daily outings as well. If something goes seriously wrong, such as one of your party becomes ill, then you will turn to them to call their doctor or take you to their hospital or call their local police, whatever is needed. If there is, God forbid, a fire in the night, then your friends will help you find the way out and probably take charge of you all. This is what children need too. They need to know that there is somebody in charge here and that they are safe and looked after with good firm boundaries to protect them and help them sort out their differences that are fair, reasonable and up for discussion — but boundaries nonetheless. This, along with their personal freedom and the ability to be away from the adults, makes the good environment for raising a family.

Laugh a lot, make jokes, get mad sometimes, have a lot of fun, a bit of light teasing and a few tears. Things do not always go perfectly all the time — that is life! Together you can get through it by looking at things with calm maturity and always love, laughter, and support for each other; brought up this way, there is less likelihood of major problems. All the brothers and sisters will grow to be the closest friends, though there will be plenty of arguments on the way! Your children will fundamentally be calm, dignified, thoughtful, and fun-loving — just the sort of people the world needs!

Where do we go from here?

Many years ago, I wrote a poem which I called 'The Sadness'. It was about how wonderful it has been to have children and the lovely things we have done and enjoyed, just like most other families.

It went on to say that, as a parent, I am always carrying a sadness that will never go away. This is even though my family are now grown-up and living their adult lives and I see them often, enjoy a lovely rounded extended family life and am so, so proud of what they have become. It is a sadness that they are not my little ones anymore. It is a sadness that all parents will carry and one that we have to learn to accept much earlier on than we anticipated — not when our children leave to go to college or to travel, but when they are four or five or six and need space and freedom to be themselves.

It can be a difficult one initially, but we have to find ways of getting along with our own lives and enjoying who we are as people and not always as parents. I remember that weird feeling when my babies were growing up and I started going out for walks or to the shops without a pushchair or pram. It was quite frightening to find that I was beginning to have to justify myself as an individual person and not just as a mum. Naturally, we all find ways of doing this and come out the other side all in one piece, but it can be a bit of a difficult one to deal with. A good friend of mine got a dog and unashamedly heaped love and attention upon it whilst openly laughing about the fact that it was a baby substitute!

I remember once standing in the queue at the supermarket, hearing a child crying and looking down to see that I was gently rocking my trolley back and forth. Oh dear!

We do, however, need to address this sadness, because for many of us, no matter how much we love and enjoy our children as adults and get to cuddle our grandchildren, and no matter how often we see them, the truth is that in the end what we want is to be cuddled up on our sofa with our little babies again, watching TV, giggling and dropping chocolate on our pyjamas.

So, I will say it loudly for the final time. Our children do not belong to us and they owe us nothing. They are not here for us to 'own', but here for themselves, and we cannot impair their lives with our own hang-ups, selfish wishes or needs, though hopefully, we can manage our lives in such a way that we can have all the fun that we can during the family journey and forever afterwards.

We have to let them go and to take enormous satisfaction in the fact that we have given them every chance to be happy and well-balanced individuals who will, in turn, be wonderful partners, parents and kind-hearted, responsible community members who will care for our dear world and help it thrive.

Our children do not belong to us and they owe us nothing.

We have to let them go.

Conclusion
Finding the right balance

The raising of children can cover a broad age range and as well as a wide range of previous experiences and child-rearing philosophies. I am aware that what I have been writing has not been directed at any particular age of child. So, I could have been talking to a dad of a child of three or a mum of a teenager or both.

It might be that somebody picking this book up will have followed a regime of quite disciplined relationships with their children, or on the other hand, they might be very, very liberal in the way they approach things.

For example, I heard from some parents in China who, after bringing her up in a very conventional way, began to see that their 13-year-old daughter was unhappy in the mainstream education system and family structure, so they had taken to reading about psychology. Through this, they had found my father's books and had loved what they were reading. They decided that they would change their whole approach to their daughter and her rights to equality in the family and offered her more freedom. After a year of success in this, though it had been slow progress, they asked if she could attend Summerhill. So, these people had come from a very harsh regime of child-rearing into a more 'Summerhill' approach, and so far, they are very happy with it.

On the other hand, I had a mail last year from a young woman in India who had been reading a lot about freedom for children. She was desperate. Her three-year-old daughter was completely out of control. She went to bed when she wanted to, slept where she wanted to and was fractious and overtired a lot of the day. She would not eat at any given time, and she watched TV and played on her computer almost all day.

I wrote to her laying out precisely what I felt was going wrong, urging her to get a good steady routine and some family systems in place and to stop allowing her daughter to rule the roost. I later received a mail to say that things were going a lot better now that she had started a more structured management in the family (also that her partner, who had not agreed with the first regime at all, was very relieved indeed!).

So, we can see from this that parents come from very far extremes, and it is difficult to offer advice without knowing what sort of background we are talking about. We also see that it is never too late to make changes. This can be discussed and talked over with older children, but with younger ones, it can just happen and evolve.

This is not a manual of child-rearing, nor an instruction book. I have tried to put down my thoughts and experiences from Summerhill and my home and hope that readers may find at least part of it valuable. I do not want to tell people how to rear their families — but I have seen an awful lot of children and families over an extensive range of years and in a unique environment.

Whether or not you are wrestling with parenting or know somebody who is struggling themselves, then there might be some small part of these chapters that you find helpful.

Thank you for your time in reading this book.

Zoë Neill Readhead,
Summerhill School, Suffolk UK
Summer 2021

Index